A Kingdom of Their Own

The Story of The Palmers of Glen Eyrie

Stephen J. May

GLEN EYRIE.

GLEN EYRIE.

A KINGDOM OF THEIR OWN
Published by Glen Eyrie
3820 North 30th Street
Colorado Springs, CO 80904
719-272-7410
www.gleneyrie.org

Cover image: John Singer Sargent (1856–1925), Portrait of Miss Elsie Palmer (A Lady in White), 1889–1890, oil on canvas. Funds acquired through public subscription and Debutante Ball Purchase Funds, FA1969.3. Collection of the Colorado Springs Fine Arts Center.

ISBN 978-0-692-89681-5

1   2   3   4   5   6   7   8   9

Permission granted by Stephen J. May to The Navigators, dba. Glen Eyrie to print this edition, 2017

Cover Design and Interior Layout: Rob Ladefoged

Cover image: John Singer Sargent (1856–1925), Portrait of Miss Elsie Palmer (A Lady in White), 1889–1890, oil on canvas. Funds acquired through public subscription and Debutante Ball Purchase Funds, FA1969.3. Collection of the Colorado Springs Fine Arts Center.

Printed in the United States of America

To Marcus Costantino,

who believed

"There is no present or future,
only the past happening again and again, now."

—Eugene O'Neill

Contents

Preface

Several years ago I had the privilege of writing a monthly feature article titled "Speaking of Art" for Southwest Art. At the time I was also teaching college courses in the history of art and literature. My goal in writing the articles was to provide the reader with historical context and analysis of important works of art and hopefully explain why they were memorable.

I was living and working in Colorado Springs at the time, a city rich in history and culture. One magazine assignment took me to the Colorado Springs Fine Arts Center, where I encountered the *Portrait of Miss Elsie Palmer* by the noted artist, John Singer Sargent, one of the great portrait painters in the history of art. I was mesmerized by it. I still am, and it became the inspiration for this book. Perhaps it is the way Sargent posed the reluctant seventeen-year-old against the Tudor linen-fold screen, or the way Elsie's figure sits so gracefully still, or the manner in which she beams so brightly and so cozily in her elegant dress, like a brisk cup of English tea. The eyes are another story. As I will discuss in the book, Sargent took great care to get the expression just right and to probe into her remarkable character and personality.

The painting became my introduction to the Palmer family. In this book I used all the available evidence to tell the story of the Palmer family. Several good books have discussed William Jackson Palmer and Queen Palmer's life, but this book introduces the reader to the Palmer as a family unit: their ambitions, travels, separations, longings, and accomplishments. I have concentrated on William Palmer's emotional, cultural, and family life instead of his business days developing railroads in the West. Other writers have covered his business life in great detail, and so I saw no reason to duplicate their fine efforts. In addition to Will and Queen, I examine the lives of their three daughters: Elsie, Dorothy, and Marjory. My goal was to give as much time and space to all the family members and balance this with General Palmer's distinguished career.

The other "member" of the family, as it were, is their home—Glen Eyrie, the stately English Tudor-style castle nestled in a canyon below Pikes Peak. As I explain in the following pages, the plan and construction of the home paralleled the exciting and sometimes tragic lives of its inhabitants. As a result, Glen Eyrie emerges with a personality all its own.

In the process of writing this book I discovered two extraordinary individuals: Will and Queen Palmer. In his lifetime, William Jackson Palmer, Civil War hero and founder of Colorado Springs, discouraged biographies of himself and in fact left little of his personal life behind. His legacy survives in his letters and written documents. Queen Palmer has been unfairly maligned by some historians, and I hope to correct that image. Her fragile health dealt her a difficult hand and it caused her to make decisions she might have avoided had she been healthy. Nonetheless, she was a brave woman, placing her family many times above her own personal ambitions.

Will and Queen were not without their flaws—they had their disagreements and minor disputes. They often went their separate ways, but retained a deep respect and love for each other. Here will you find no scandal, double dealing, back stabbing, or revenge, but the story of a fascinating couple and their children who carved a life and a home out of the rugged canyon country of the Rockies—a kingdom of their own.

I am indebted to several institutions in the preparation and writing of this book: the Pikes Peak Library District, Tutt Library, the Navigators Archives, the Colorado Springs Fine Arts Center, and particularly the Starsmore Center for Local History at the Colorado

Springs Pioneers Museum. I would like to thank Assistant Archivist Stephanie Prochaska of the Starsmore Center for her help in screening and selecting materials and images for inclusion in the book.

The Horse Soldier

History often has a way of overlooking the deeds of great men. Consider the military career of William Jackson Palmer. Fighting for Union forces during the Civil War and engaging in several important battles, he was promoted to the rank of brevet brigadier general before he reached thirty years of age and went on to receive the Medal of Honor for heroism. He was handsome in a masculine way and a decisive commander; he demonstrated great courage and fortitude on the Front lines. He could be bold and headstrong in certain situations, but his men followed his commands implicitly. He had most of the admirable qualities of great men, except he did not have the idiosyncrasies that most often lead to fame. He lacked Custer's flamboyance, Burnside's sideburns, Sherman's iron will, McClellan's sloth, Lee's battlefield brilliance, or Grant's grizzled perseverance. He had noble character, but it was without flash or verve. Despite his valorous military career, his reputation was overshadowed by his life as a builder of railroads and his role in founding Colorado Springs.

Like many great men, Palmer rose from austere and modest beginnings. He was born on September 16, 1836, on Kinsale Farm, Kent County, Delaware, to John and Matilda Palmer, who were dedicated members of the Hicksite sect of Quakers. As opposed to the more conservative Orthodox sect, the Hicksites stressed that divinity was in every man and that behavior was more important than a set of principles to follow strictly. The Hicksites steered away from a formal application of the scriptures and instead promoted a belief that moral decisions could be accomplished by following one's "inner light." This inner light principle helped Palmer navigate a nineteenth century filled with complexity, uncertainty, and contradiction.

Abolition was at the forefront of all Quakers' beliefs. In the latter part of the eighteenth century, the Quakers of England struggled to end the Atlantic slave trade and the subsequent emancipation of all slaves. In 1807, after decades of bitter, violent struggle, the ban on the transportation of slaves was made official in British Parliament. Without the direct involvement of the Quakers, such an event might have been delayed by as much as a decade. In America, both Hicksite and Orthodox Quakers fought at every turn for abolition. After the Palmer family moved to Germantown near Philadelphia in 1841, the cries for the elimination of slavery were heard throughout the Friends meeting houses and in the streets.

In the 1840s, a maturing Will Palmer felt the agitation and excitement of antebellum Philadelphia. Anti-Catholic riots were followed by abolition riots. In August of 1842, the African Presbyterian Church was burned to the ground. In the ensuing years, other mysterious church burnings were reported. Immigrants from Germany, Britain, and Ireland flooded in. Railroads extended their lines in and out of town. In 1846, town criers called for military volunteers in the newly declared war with Mexico.

The Palmers lived in a modest two-story house on High Street in Germantown. After attending Zane Street Grammar School, Will entered Central High School of Philadelphia at the age of twelve. His curriculum included the customary preparatory subjects of writing and mathematics, plus courses in surveying, navigation, and natural sciences; his education at home consisted of lessons in Quaker values, personal integrity, responsibility for one's actions, and above all service to others.

In 1853, when he was seventeen, Palmer joined the Hempfield railroad as a surveyor. The railroad was running its tracks through the rugged hill country west of the Allegheny Mountains, hoping to join the vast network of tracks that extended throughout Pennsylvania and New York.

It was exhausting but exhilarating work. Palmer thrived in the mountains, as they provided a thrilling counterpoint to the dissension in Philadelphia. He cooked venison by the side of the tracks, washed down by hot black coffee or clear mountain spring water. At night he crawled between two tarpaulins and watched the stars pulse and fade before sleep. If the crew was lucky they could put up for the night in a small roadside inn, where eight to twelve overworked men collapsed and slept in the same room. He made friends with the engineers and firemen aboard the big high-wheeled, narrow gauge locomotives, thrilled by their belching and snorting as they moved along the tracks.

It was here on the surveying crews one week that opportunity cried out to Will. Early locomotives burned cordwood, a dense hardwood that reached high temperatures. Firemen were kept constantly busy feeding wood into the burners. Clouds of greasy black smoke poured from the smokestacks, choking workers and passengers alike. The amount of wood needed to power locomotives called for vast amounts of timber to be felled and stacked by the side of the tracks. Palmer wondered if a better, more efficient source of fuel could be used. He knew that coal was being burned experimentally in certain lines and that right there in Pennsylvania there were mountains of fossil fuel deposits.

The idea of coal-burning locomotives continued to interest him. Palmer's uncle, Frank Jackson, who worked for the Westmoreland Coal Company, suggested that Palmer find out first hand by visiting Great Britain to discover how the English successfully used coal in the development of their vast railroad empire. In 1855, after his uncle lent him the money, Will Palmer sailed to Southampton to test the viability of his ideas. Sailing aboard the Tuscarora and supping on ground biscuits and pork fat, the landlubber Palmer had to quickly grow his sea legs. In mid-Atlantic the ocean got ugly, as the wind-whipped foam and spume roared over the foredeck and tossed around crew and passengers. He hunkered down in the steerage section, where he shared his passage with one hundred and twenty-five other souls trying to get to England. Finally the sea calmed, the sun broke through, and the wind dropped. "I do not think I could have seen more life in a little compass anywhere else as well as I have done in the two weeks in the packet ship. The day has been another splendid one," he wrote in a letter, "and the Tuscarora, under the influence of a 7-knot breeze, flies along to everyone's satisfaction. But I am called away by the cry of 'a whale, a whale' and put away hastily my portfolio."[1]

After arriving in England, Palmer prepared to cover the island kingdom from one corner to the other, experiencing the life in the mines, factories, and railroads. He quickly became educated in alternative railroad methods, particularly in the distinct advantages of burning coal over wood and the use of the narrow gauge, then gaining popularity in Great Britain. Palmer filled a journal with his observations, convinced as he was that the British held the key to Americans one day building a transcontinental railroad. Coal was the only answer to the long-range ambitions of railroad men; the narrow gauge provided the answer for locomotives negotiating tight, hairpin, mountain slopes.[2]

On his journeys Palmer developed over time as a writer with a fairly strong narrative and descriptive sense. He was at his best when he stuck to direct observation rather than yielding to the temptation to soar into flights of fancy, his prose turning decidedly purple. Before leaving America, he had arranged to write articles for the Miner's Journal in Pottsville, Pennsylvania, and so he fed his readers back home a stream of provocative stories on customs, morays, and the difficulties of foreign travel. In his letters to his family and friends he used the terms "thee" and "thine" in the Quaker tradition.

At one point in his journey he encountered some British stodginess. He was expected to have a letter of recommendation when visiting businesses in England. When Palmer knocked on the door of a London soap maker without such a letter, he was turned away by the owner. Miffed by the rejection, he left a wiser man about foreign customs. Despite his bad experiences with English manners and customs, and in most cases because of them, he revered English society, to the degree he would become an ardent Anglophile.

Upon his return to Philadelphia in 1856, promotions happened quickly for Palmer. He joined the Westmoreland Coal Company and in June 1857 he accepted the position of private secretary to J. Edgar

Thomson, president of the Pennsylvania Railroad, who groomed the twenty-year-old Palmer in the business of running a railroad. He employed what he learned surveying in western Pennsylvania and his experiences in Great Britain.

But events beyond Pennsylvania were conspiring to derail his ambitions, as the prospect of civil war loomed on the horizon.

In the summer of 1859, Philadelphia felt the tension of the impending crisis. Pro-slavery and anti-slavery forces clashed in the sultry August streets. With a Quaker friend of his named Isaac Clothier, Will organized a series of lectures under the obscure title *The Young Men's Liberal Course of Lectures*, which would address the slavery issue and offer significant abolitionists the chance to speak before large Philadelphia audiences in National Hall. Notable speakers such as Lucretia Mott and Wendell Phillips signed up to attend. Through the latter part of 1859, the audiences continued to grow, the rhetoric increasing in pitch and intensity. Outside the hall, angry crowds gathered and often threatened to barge in on the proceedings. Keeping them under some order was usually a ring of policemen armed with billy clubs.

The lectures continued through the fall of 1859, but on October 16, white abolitionist John Brown attacked the armory at Harper's Ferry, Virginia, hoping to incite a slave revolt and race war. Brown was executed on December 2 in a highly sensationalized public hanging. Seething with unrest, the country reacted to this shocking development. The police force in Philadelphia was put on notice, its ranks swelling to over six hundred officers. On December 15, with Clothier and Palmer in attendance, the lecture in National Hall went on as scheduled. As furious crowds gathered outside, organizers considered canceling the event, but Palmer and Clothier disagreed. "We felt we had no right to do that," Clothier admitted later. "It would be pandering to the passions of the mob and a surrender of free speech."[3]

Outside, six hundred policemen with loaded revolvers kept dissenters from entering. Speakers and attendees that night included abolitionist notables Lucretia Mott, Mary Grew, Charles Wise, and Clement Biddle, among others. Some protesters had filtered into the hall, and as speakers rose, contentious howls rippled through the crowd. "Rough looking men jumped up on benches and gave cheers for the Union, to drown the voice of the lecturer," noted Clothier. "The police rushed at them, seized them, and carried them out through a doorway under the platform."[4] The protesters were locked in an empty freight car and the lectures continued, punctuated here and there with sporadic shouts and screaming catcalls. As the evening ended, both Clothier and Palmer congratulated each other—their cause had been vindicated and free speech had been victorious.

After Fort Sumter surrendered to Confederate forces on April 14, events moved swiftly and decisively. President Lincoln authorized calling up 75,000 volunteers to "put down combinations of too powerful to be suppressed by the ordinary course of judicial proceedings." On April 17, Virginia voted to secede from the Union and join the Confederacy.[5] Other southern states quickly followed.

Tensions escalated through the early summer of 1861. America had not fought a major war since 1846, but the struggle with Mexico was hardly more than a skirmish compared to the looming conflict between the North and the South. Mostly drawn from farms and factories, volunteers were ill equipped, poorly trained, insufficiently clothed, and in some cases barely literate. This rabble in arms, on both sides, was soon organized into companies and regiments, drilled, and moved to the Front lines where, initially, they were thrown into battle and scarcely able to distinguish their comrades from the enemy. This was particularly true during the first major battle of the war, First Bull Run, in July 1861, fought near Manassas, Virginia, in which Lincoln's hand-picked commander, General Irwin McDowell, led his 18,000-man army against a similar-sized Confederate force. William Palmer, as well as many Union sympathizers, was shocked by the Confederate victory, to the degree that the battle and its aftermath convinced him to join the army. If the Union was to be saved and slavery abolished, it would take men like him to volunteer his time and put his convictions on the line. Fiercely idealistic, Palmer wrestled with his moral conscience for several days. Should he take up arms and thereby renounce the pacifist principles that he had lived with all his short life? Should he kill other men for the sake of a righteous cause? Was the issue of slavery and its abolition enough to sway his decision? He turned to his belief in inner light for his ultimate decision. Deciding the Union cause was just, he organized a confident band of northern forces (mostly fellow Quakers), known as the Anderson troop, which slowly expanded into the more formidable Fifteenth Pennsylvania Cavalry.

Although Palmer believed his course of action was right, his parents did not. A year into the war, his father wrote to him: "I can never feel that any love or admiration for the profession thee has thought it in thy duty to engage in, and our fervent hope is that there may have no opportunity to distinguish thyself or to acquire any honor on that most horrible of all earthly scenes—a field of battle."[6] In another letter John and Matilda detailed their meager family living expenses and urged him to come home and help out. "Resign, come home," they pleaded. "Leave the army and enter into some useful business in civil life. The rebellion is virtually ended here. Thee can be of more use to thy country tenfold in this way than thee can ever become as a soldier." Despite their entreaties, Palmer held firm.[7]

Captain Palmer's unit was assigned to Major General McClellan's Army of the Potomac during the vicious and costly battle of Antietam in mid-September 1862. Palmer, twenty-five years old, was five foot nine, thin as a sapling and sported a clean-shaven face. Later he cultivated a generous mustache several shades lighter than his chestnut-colored hair.

Palmer liked the cavalry for several reasons. "There is something about the cavalry," he wrote, "that accords with my spirit than the other arms."[8] He enjoyed the camaraderie of his fellow horsemen and the sight and smell of a cavalry unit in battle. He developed a riding style that others described as reckless, a style that allowed his legs less grip on the ribs of the horse and his feet more freedom in the stirrups. Consequently it made him more vulnerable to spills. To his credit and much to his riding ability, Palmer rode accident free through the Civil War. The cavalry still had a romantic image to the country, which did much to encourage the idea that war was still a gallant affair waged by noble warriors.

From Alexander the Great down to Napoleon and Wellington, mounted horsemen were an integral part of an army. The sight of advancing cavalry, with guidons flying and bugles blaring, instilled fear and panic in the most courageous of infantrymen. When war arrived in America, the cavalry relied less on frontal assaults and more on reconnaissance missions, harassment of the enemy, tracking army units, and ferreting out southern sympathizers. In many people's minds, the Confederate cavalry, because of the men's traditional rural backgrounds, were superior to their Union counterparts. In the early days of the war, however, the Union cavalry enjoyed widespread support and popularity.

Both Union and Confederate forces faced grim conditions in their respective camps. Pay was fifteen dollars per day. If one was wealthy enough one could avoid service by paying a substitute to fight for him. Disease and malnutrition stalked the camps. Officers had to rouse platoons and companies of ill fed and poorly clothed men, some without shoes, and prepare them for battle.

Drinking, prostitution, and gambling alleviated some of the conditions on the battle lines, but soldiers endured hours and days waiting for the sound of guns to go into the conflict. As the war advanced, desertions spiked. Despite the sordid conditions, both sides fought with bravery and extraordinary courage in the face of withering gunfire.

The Fifteenth Pennsylvania had several minor skirmishes until the crucial battle of Shiloh in April 1862, after which Will's zeal for war seemed to evaporate. He wrote to his uncle:

> I would like to describe the battlefield to you—on which the dead lay thick, our present encampment being almost literally fenced around with the unburied bodies of men and horses— and some of the scenes in the wood that skirts us giving me as vivid impression of the horrors of battle as it would be possible to gain. But I have no taste to describe, and you have probably none to read of such things. As I gazed yesterday afternoon

upon a little area in the adjoining woods, on which the dead and disfigured rebel bodies lay more than usually thick, some of them being charred in the most repulsive manner by fire, the shells having ignited the underbrush, my mind reverted to the handful of Congressional and legislative conspirators whose plottings last winter had ultimated in scenes like this ... and I thought there must surely be some dire punishment for them, to avenge scenes like this ... I'll write some other time and show you how little of a science war is, as conducted by our "distinguished generals."[9]

As the months passed, the fighting intensified and casualties escalated. The battle of Antietam demonstrated the limitations of the cavalry for both sides, as close-quarter fighting and volleys of musket fire made it virtually useless in battle. In September of 1862, General Lee and his army of 18,000 men crossed the Potomac, hoping to gain a foothold in northern territory. Attempting to repulse them was General McClellan's 65,000-man army, dug in near Antietam Creek, Maryland.

The two armies mauled each other the entire day of the seventeenth. The Union cavalry under Major General Ambrose Burnside attempted to break through the Confederate lines by seizing a stone bridge across Antietam Creek. The attack was partially successful until a counterattack by Confederate Brigadier General A.P. Hill in the afternoon turned back the Union advance. In the meantime, the action turned deadly for both sides. In the nearby cornfield, knots of men clashed in hand-to-hand fighting. Soldiers beat each other with rifle butts and lunged with bayonets. Officers on horseback screamed orders that no one could hear in the din. Rifles jammed from the heat. Thick bands of light and dark gray smoke clogged the battlefield. "The battle sounded like a swarm of angry bees," wrote Corporal John Phelps of Palmer's regiment. "We sat there and listened. Sometimes it was like innumerable voices of men angry at something being done that they didn't like. The leaves of the trees were all vibrating."[10] By late afternoon and into the evening, the dead were strewn across a mile of meadowland, along the creek bank and up the hills. Both sides took 22,000 casualties that day, the bloodiest one-day conflict in American history. Although it was not a clear win for either side, Confederate forces were first to withdraw and so the Union was quick to claim victory. Although Will Jackson was not directly involved in the cavalry skirmish, his unit was ordered to mop up operations by rounding up any Confederate stragglers, interrogating them, and securing the area around Antietam Creek and nearby Sharpsburg.

After the battle, on September 18, the late summer sun revealed McClellan's battle-weary army bivouacked along a string of burnished hills near Sharpsburg, Maryland. Pockets of smoke still drifted in the motionless air. Several miles away, its back to the Potomac River and Virginia, Lee's similarly exhausted army camped and nursed its wounded. During the course of the morning, McClellan summoned Captain Palmer to his command tent. Palmer raised the canvas flap and quickly noticed a map stretched out on a folding table in front of McClellan. Too emotionally spent for pleasantries, McClellan ordered Palmer on an intelligence-gathering mission behind enemy lines. Palmer, chafing for action, which he later described as "a fit of injudicious patriotism," relished the idea.[11]

McClellan's goal was to ascertain that General Lee's army was indeed retreating and would pose no present threat to Union forces in Maryland. McClellan also recruited I.L. Stine, a Lutheran pastor and sometime espionage agent, to join Palmer in the mission. Because of his Quaker upbringing and his natural pacifist leanings, Palmer disliked the thick of battle. Therefore, this moment of derring-do strongly appealed to his nature. Wearing civilian clothes, they left at dusk, crossing the Potomac River and into Virginia. "There was no moon that night," noted Palmer, "and the starlight was partially obscured by a warm mist; yet it was light enough to distinguish objects moving on the opposite shore, while the air was so quiet that the chants of katydids could be distinctly heard across the stream."[12] They picked their way to a farmhouse close to the border until they were intercepted by a Confederate mounted patrol. Stine managed to slip away, but Palmer was captured and brought to the headquarters of General William Pendleton, Lee's chief of artillery. The cool-headed Palmer introduced himself as W.J. Peters, an engineer inspecting mines in the area. Pendleton saw quickly through Palmer's subterfuge and had him detained. After some deliberation about what to do with this Union spy, Pendleton decided to ship Palmer to Castle Thunder prison in Richmond.

Variously described as "infamous," "notorious," and "unendurable," Castle Thunder was a Union soldier's worse nightmare. The prison was actually three brick buildings in the heart of Richmond that were commandeered by the Confederacy: Gleanor's Tobacco Factory, Whitlock's Warehouse, and Palmer's Factory. Gleanor's was reserved for Confederate spies and political prisoners; Whitlock's housed black and female inmates; and Palmer's—ironically—held Union spies and prisoners of war. A twelve-foot wall surrounded the three prisons. Captain Palmer was soon tossed into a cell where he would spend the next four months. During that time, the fourteen hundred-inmate capacity swelled to three thousand. Dysentery and smallpox decimated the ranks, but Palmer, either through good genes or proper sanitation, managed to avoid any fatal illnesses. Unauthorized lashings in the yard were common, as were the daily rounds of the commandant, Captain George Alexander, who was usually accompanied by his vicious dog, Nero, to keep prisoners in line.

His imprisonment lasted from September 19 to January 15, 1863, and would have been shortened if his daring escape had been successful. Within weeks of his captivity, Palmer and his cellmate began tunneling to freedom. Every day they sawed a section of floor with a knife under one of the beds. While Palmer sawed, his cellmate shuffled his feet to cover the noise. Hours were spent sawing through the boards. When they finally broke through they lowered themselves into the crawl space that led to freedom on the other side. But just as they saw the light, duty guards shoved rifle barrels into their faces. Their escape thwarted, Palmer resigned himself to miserable days of captivity.

After losing twenty pounds but none of his patriotism, Palmer was soon released to his regiment in a prisoner exchange and was promoted to colonel. Before joining his unit, he recuperated for two weeks, writing letters and recounting his prison ordeal to interested ears. He was then sent west to Tennessee to rejoin his regiment and ostensibly to restore leadership to its shattered ranks.

Palmer was immediately greeted with the news that nearly six hundred of his men were being detained for mutiny. During the battle of Murfreesboro, they had refused an order to charge the Confederate lines. Later, they cited a lack of commissioned and noncommissioned officers as a major reason for their unwillingness to do battle—a rather flimsy excuse given the gravity of their actions. "I pity the poor fellows who mutinied," Palmer wrote, "so many of them are led into it without reflection and in that careless accidental way by which it is so easy to stray from the right path into the wrong."[13] Three top commissioned officers had been killed at Murfreesboro, leaving a regiment demoralized and badly in need of leadership.

Colonel Palmer assumed command while the mutiny was under investigation in Washington. In a few short weeks he managed to reorganize his regiment, restore discipline, and negotiate partial clemency for his six hundred mutineers. They were spared death by firing squad through Palmer's intervention.

Palmer's experiences through the duration of the war are recorded in the annals of the Fifteenth Pennsylvania Cavalry. His faultless performance as commander caught the eye of Major General George H. Thomas, who recommended Palmer for promotion to brevet brigadier general, a singular honor given that the colonel was barely twenty-eight years of age. Only he and George Armstrong Custer received a one-star general rank during the war before the age of thirty.

On January 14, 1865, three months before the war's end, General Palmer's cavalry crept forward to the wooded rise of a small hill overlooking Red

Brigadier General William Jackson Palmer, 1865. Palmer was one of the youngest brigadier generals in the army at the time. Courtesy of the Starsmore Center for Local History, Colorado Springs Pioneers Museum.

Hill, Alabama. It was just after sunrise, the air still frosty, the horses snorting and nibbling at their bits. The horses moved into position, their riders checking their carbines at the crest of the hill. Palmer waited to give the command. Below them a camp of several hundred Confederate soldiers lay unaware of the Union advance. Palmer glanced left and right, assuring that every trooper was ready for the attack. Palmer's voice shattered the still morning air. Horses and riders leaped from the hilltop, the riders' sabers flashing momentarily in the sun. They charged down into the ravine where the enemy lay. Palmer bolted ahead, his pistol raised in the air and urging on his men.

A fierce battle ensued. The Confederates had been caught napping as the Pennsylvania cavalry charged through the camp, killing retaliating soldiers and capturing the rest. His soldiers rounded up the prisoners and Palmer surveyed his losses. To his astonishment, not one of his men had been killed, while his unit captured over two hundred Confederate soldiers. For his actions, he was awarded the Medal of Honor (bestowed in 1894).

After Abraham Lincoln's assassination in April 1865 and the collapse of the South, Palmer and his unit were ordered to pursue Confederate President Jefferson Davis as he fled through the Carolinas and Georgia. Union government officials had also implicated Davis in Lincoln's assassination, so there was an additional reason to capture Davis and bring him to trial. Devastated by Lincoln's death, Palmer was absolutely dogged in the chase, driving his men through dense thickets, ravaged cornfields, scorched hamlets, and forests heavy with spring growth. "I am now hunting him at every crossroad, ferry, and bridge," he wrote home. Although Palmer did not find Davis, he and his unit were credited with driving him into the hands of Union Major General James Wilson, who captured Davis on May 10, near Irwinville, Georgia.[14]

After the armistice at Appomattox, most soldiers, including Palmer, were too scarred by war or exhausted to display much enthusiasm for the ensuing peace. Mustered out of the army in Nashville, Tennessee, in mid-June 1865, Palmer grabbed his bags and headed to the station to take the train to Philadelphia. He was twenty-eight and ready to resume his charmed life.

But he soon realized that his life would not take shape in Philadelphia, or anywhere in the East for that matter. Since the end of the war, the talk was all about the West: its opportunities, its economic lures, its boundless resources. The Pacific Railway act of 1862 had authorized the building of a transcontinental railroad. The war had interrupted its progress, but with the coming of peace, a renewed push to join the coasts was underway. Palmer wished to be a part of this post-war America and help lay the track to the Rockies through Kansas. "I often find myself doubting that a kind Providence ever intended man to dwell on the Atlantic slope," he once wrote.[15] Hired as a construction manager for the Kansas Pacific Railroad, Palmer and his assistant, Edward Johnson, left Philadelphia for St. Louis in 1867 to begin his duties. Three years before his marriage to Mary Lincoln Mellen and five years before the birth of his first daughter, Elsie, Palmer headed West along with a vanguard of other visionary, ambitious men.

Railroad men pride themselves on their visible accomplishments. While explorers and mountain men have their tracks covered by the wind and shifting sands, the men who established the vast train networks could look with satisfaction at the miles of track they helped to create. For Palmer, such an enterprise blessed his daily life, as once again he returned to his life with the railroad.

In 1867, he was hired by the Kansas Pacific Railroad to survey the best route from Kansas to the Pacific Coast. The more monumental the task, the more Palmer seemed to enjoy it. Traveling on horseback and leading mules, Palmer led his survey party to the Rockies and then on to San Francisco, roughly following the thirty-fifth parallel through present day New Mexico and Arizona. He covered four thousand miles and his notations and observations established the groundwork for the railroad track to be laid. On his journey he became acquainted with a British doctor, William Bell, who was assigned the job of photographing the expedition. Initially Bell knew nothing about photography, but after a two-week crash course, he joined the party in western Kansas. Bell and Palmer quickly became comrades; Bell would later become a successful investor in several of Palmer's ventures.

"Willie" Bell was five years younger than Palmer, thoroughly English, a Cambridge University graduate, a man who liked to dunk his toast in a hot cup of tea promptly at four in the afternoon. Although a novice at photography, he took his job seriously. Bell and Palmer encountered a Kansas-Colorado border aflame with violence. A little less than three years before, Colonel John Chivington and a seven hundred–man militia had massacred a Cheyenne and Arapahoe village at Sand Creek in eastern Colorado. Since that time, Indian bands had retaliated against whites in the area, especially against cavalry patrols and in the late 1860s against crews laying railroad tracks through their lands. On June 26, 1867, while working with the survey crew, Bell photographed the scalped and mutilated body of trooper Sergeant Frederick Wyllyams of the Seventh Cavalry near Fort Wallace, Kansas. After the photograph was published in *Harper's Weekly*, railroad officials became concerned that Bell might wish to capitalize on the venture for himself. Nevertheless, Bell continued on with Palmer's expedition, an expedition that he later chronicled in his popular book, *New Tracks in North America* (1869).

In Kansas Bell described the tedious methods of the survey crew:

> At Fort Wallace the transit-man, leveler, and topographer of each division had obtained mules and one of the wagons had been emptied of its contents and devoted, for a time, to the surveyors. One division commenced work, and the men were soon spread out into a line a mile long upon the plain, measuring and taking observations at every point. On one side of this line came the wagons, following each other closely, and guarded by a small body of the escort. The remainder of the cavalry moved with surveyors, some in front, others in the rear, the greater number in the center ... The transit man, carrying his instruments on his shoulders, and riding a mule at a gallop, would suddenly stop, jump off, arrange the transit, wave to the flag man ahead, wait until satisfied of the correctness of his observations, then back into the saddle,

shoulder his transit, and gallop away again. Behind him came the road men and levelers, mounted in the same way and advancing with a like rapid accuracy."[16]

In addition to Palmer and Bell, the crew consisted of three teams totaling forty-eight engineers and a staff of ten. A troop of cavalry served as escort from Kansas to Trinidad, Colorado. The crew surveyed the area of Raton Pass, the gateway to Santa Fe and the lands of the Pueblos. In northern New Mexico, Palmer halted his company at the ranch of Lucien Maxwell, where for a long afternoon the two discussed the future of the territory. The size of Maxwell's property—one of the largest land grants in the country—was extensive: two and half times the size of Rhode Island. Palmer knew that if the Kansas Pacific put its tracks through this area, it would have to negotiate with Maxwell for rights of way. Additionally, Palmer eyed the territory for a future rail line from Denver to Mexico City.

As he traveled through the West, Palmer discovered that his impeccable credentials allowed him access to important people. Retiring as a brigadier general and being a veteran of Shiloh and Antietam were singular honors that carried great weight in the country. Although many men and women might have expected a wizened fellow with a limp and graying, mutton-chopped side whiskers, they quickly found a strapping thirty-year-old with towering ambitions.

Often the party split up to gain a more accurate lay of the land. Searing July and August temperatures reached ninety-five degrees as the men reached present day Albuquerque and headed west to Arizona territory. As group commander, Palmer resorted to the same discipline that had gotten him through the war. The men adjusted to it, and even adapted to Palmer barking orders.

The landscape turned arid and bleak. The earth in the rising heat became like brushed copper with patches of greasewood and mesquite. Dust, kicked up by fierce winds, blasted their faces. Swarms of flies menaced man and beast alike. A line of mountains far to the northwest rose pale blue in the withering heat. Just before nightfall they would circle the wagons, make camp, start the fires, and reminisce about the day. In the morning the mapmakers would start work on detailing their journey.

The group threaded its way through the lands of Zuni and Apache and entered the land below the San Francisco Peaks in Arizona territory. Bell was soon to separate from the group at Camp Grant and make his way to Mexico and then by ship to San Francisco. The remainder of the party under General Palmer, constantly stalked by Apaches, scouted the canyon country near Prescott, capital of the Arizona territory. After finding the canyon walls too steep for their mules and horses, they were obliged, "in spite of its violating the fundamental rule of Indian warfare in the mountains" to follow the bottom of the canyon to its mouth.[17] Studded with pine and piñon trees, the canyon rim was perfect cover for marauding Apaches. The group picked their way over boulders and rock shards for eight miles until they heard shots from the cliff overhead. Palmer gave the alarm and the men darted for cover.

The Apaches began sending down heavy boulders into the bed of the canyon. Pinned down, Palmer and his crew fired several volleys at the aggressors. After twenty minutes or so, Will decided to attack the Indians by scaling the slopes. He picked two or three men to accompany him. Clambering over rocks and ducking for cover occasionally, they shot their way to the top of the canyon. "How we got up," Palmer remarked, "God knows. I remember hearing a volley from below, shots fired above, Indian yells on all sides, the grating roar of the tumbling boulders as they fell, and the confused echoing calls from the canyon. Exhausted, out of breath, and wet with perspiration, boots nearly torn off and hands cut and bleeding, I sat down on the summit and looked around. Everything was quiet as death; the Indians had disappeared—melting away as suddenly and mysteriously as they had first appeared."[18]

It was Palmer's first armed skirmish since leaving the army in '65, and he wrote of it with the same passion that characterized his accounts in Virginia and Tennessee. Although he disliked violence, he could savor certain moments when he thought it was justified.

Under cover of night, the malnourished and gritty crew headed westward following a ribbon of green in the bed of a canyon. They soon came to the rich and fertile Val de Chino Valley, and from there forded the Colorado River at Needles. Along the way the general and his men made crucial notations as to the viability of carving a rail route through some of the most rugged country in the Southwest. Will noted that a proposed route could follow the thirty-fifth or thirty-third parallel, as both showed commercial possibilities. However, such precise assessments required endless hours of mapping and surveying, dividing his team into separate parties, and retracing their footsteps.

After arriving in San Francisco in late 1867, Palmer and his men took hot baths, devoured meals in the restaurant of the Cosmopolitan Hotel, and got fitted with new clothes. He kept his prized riding boots, which were badly scarred from the trek. After a brief rest and enjoying the sights of the city, they headed east by stagecoach to Salt Lake City and Cheyenne, and then by rail to St. Louis where he arrived in mid-March 1868. Palmer and his crew's precise measurements yielded a route length of 4,464 miles, and that was just the beginning of the eventual railroad structure to be built in the next few years.[19]

The West that Palmer witnessed was largely still raw and untamed. Except for a few outposts of civilization in Ogden, Salt Lake City, and Denver, the region was dotted with minor settlements and ramshackle railroad towns lining the route of the Union Pacific Railroad. The population of Denver was approaching five thousand; most people in the boom and bust town had only been there for a few years. The city's residents felt orphaned by the decision to route the transcontinental railroad through Cheyenne and southern Wyoming rather than through their own city and the Colorado Rockies.

Will discovered that the West's sun-patched and barren spaces stimulated his wild spirit and helped to clarify his moral direction. "How I seem to vibrate," he mused in a letter, "between a life of savagery and civilization. I think a certain amount of the former is good for a man, it is like a little spice in his rations, it gives a bouquet to his everyday life which might otherwise become humdrum ... On the Great Plains life seems stripped of its complexity; wood, grass and water, a few wild animals to outwit and shoot, a certain distance to march and then go into camp, a little round of daily duties, a limited number of relations with very few people ... Life has never seemed straighter to me than when ... I have been thrown on the Plains."[20]

Within two years Will Palmer was in an enviable position. He was director in charge of the construction of the railroad between Kansas City and Denver; by the following year he was monitoring the extension between Cheyenne and Denver. He still had his eyes on the Denver to Mexico City link, but that idea was far in the offing. Even though his fledgling railroad, the Denver and Rio Grande, was still in development, a few associates were beginning to use the term "tycoon" to describe him. It was an opportune time to begin a railroad, especially in the West, where goods and passengers needed transport across vast distances. As part of the engines of commerce, railroads lured private and government investors as well as entrepreneurs; most made fortunes in the process.

The great barons of wealth, who included Andrew Carnegie, Cornelius Vanderbilt, Leland Stanford, and Jay Gould, had all or at least one of their tentacles in railroads. Despite his name being casually linked to this group, Will never really belonged to it. Although he could drive a rigid bargain and employ great skill at handling people, he never truly crossed the line into deceit and predatory practices. He admitted that, "Amidst all the hot competition of this American business life there is great temptation to be a little unscrupulous."[21] Palmer developed into a brilliant organizational man. His powers to motivate his workers without provoking resentment were exceptional. He went to great lengths to ensure that those around him were essentially happy and productive in their labors. He knew the tide of civilization would follow the route of the railroads, and that's how he wished to connect people with cities and territories.

It had been ten years since Will watched hecklers shout down speakers in National Hall in Philadelphia and eight years since he took up arms in the Civil War, two events that thwarted his ambitions to continue his railroad career. Now in the early months of 1869, he would have his most formidable encounter, one that did not arrive with a glint of sabers or the smell of saddle leather, but one that would send his life in an entirely new direction.

This Above All

A trip to generate investors placed William Palmer on the Central Railroad as it traveled from St. Louis to Cincinnati one day in early 1869. Winter rains drenched the train as it headed east through the southern Illinois farmlands and patches of woodland.

Will became engaged in conversation with a man who introduced himself as William Mellen, a lawyer, whom Palmer considered a possible investor in his ambitious plan to link Colorado to Mexico. Mellen disclosed to Palmer that he had studied under Salmon P. Chase, Lincoln's former secretary of the treasury, and that he was acquainted with several British financiers who were in positions to fund exciting new business opportunities. Presently Mellen's eighteen-year-old daughter entered the railroad car and nestled beneath the wing of her father. Palmer was overcome by her presence—fascination and then instant love surged through him. For Queen Mellen, the feelings were mutual. As they journeyed on to Cincinnati, under the watchful eye of her father, Queen and Will shared their many experiences.

Mary Lincoln Mellen, known as Queen, was born in Prestonburg, Kentucky, on March 26, 1850. Although the origins of her name are unknown, it did not seem to denote any royal status her parents wished to confer on her. Her father and mother began calling her Queen in her childhood and the name stuck. The only time it posed a problem is when people thought she might be trying to be better than them. But for the most part, the name fit her perfectly and may have helped shape her personality.

Queen Palmer, 1872, the photo taken in Mexico City during her trip there with General Palmer and the Kingsleys. Courtesy of the Starsmore Center for Local History, Colorado Springs Pioneers Museum.

Prestonburg was a small town in eastern Kentucky that Palmer knew was a Confederate base during the war and spawned the Tenth Kentucky Cavalry, a unit he faced, ironically, in battle several years before. Queen's mother died of "brain fever" when she was four years old. Her father later married her mother's sister, Ellen Clark, with whom he had six more children. The family prospered in Flushing, Long Island, New York, her father ensuring that she was well educated, schooled in manners and properly introduced to the arts, especially music. At fifteen, Queen showed maturity beyond her years when she wrote in a school essay: "While the vocation of wife and mother is the most beautiful thing to which a woman can be called, it is not necessarily the only one, that one need be either useless or wretched to whom that calling does not come ... The nature of men and women being different, there are positions peculiarly adapted to each. A more calculated mind may fit a man better for public speaking, or heading an army, greater physical strength may make him capable of lifting great weights, but these are not the only posts of honor."[1] Queen remarked, "True friendship is founded on respect and esteem, not for an imaginary, but for some really fine trait in each. The confidence between friends must be entirely unlimited and unreserved."[2]

Queen's physical presence overpowered Will. Her large and beguiling eyes seemed to stare through him. Her eyes were a trait that she would pass on to her daughter, Elsie. From girlhood, people had commented on their beauty and trustworthiness. She was petite, a little over five foot in height, gentle in manner, and spoke in a sweet voice, tinged with a slight trace of her Kentucky roots. Her thick brunette hair always seemed to defy comb and brush, a characteristic that betrayed her coltish, independent nature. She was self-assured, had a strong sense of her own identity, and possessed a clear knowledge of what she wanted in life. Will would learn more about her as time went on, but this first meeting sparked an endearing love.

The couple began a brief and intense courtship. It did not seem to matter to Queen their thirteen-year age difference. After the war, women of marrying age faced a world without young men, and their marriage choices naturally included older bachelors and widowers. Their age difference may have motivated her even more to demonstrate to Will her maturity and values. She was of course swept away by her suitor. Not many women could claim to be in love with a Civil War general, western explorer, and railroad entrepreneur. Will on the other hand reveled in her attention and used his valorous experiences to encourage the relationship.

Through her youth and adolescence, Queen developed a love of the arts. From the borough in Queens, New York, her family frequented the Brooklyn Museum, where she could attain an education in painting and sculpture. Prior to the debut of the Metropolitan Museum of Art in 1872, the Brooklyn Museum offered art-hungry New Yorkers the opportunity to see European and American masters. Hals and van Dyck as well as more contemporary American artists such as Samuel Morse and Frederick Church were well represented. Queen honed her critical skills in the halls of the Brooklyn Museum while appreciating some of the individual qualities of each artist.

The couple met during the waning months of the Andrew Johnson administration and the days prior to the inauguration on March 4 of President-elect Ulysses S. Grant, Palmer's former commander in chief. To the relief of many, the Johnson years were over, marked by corruption and a highly publicized impeachment trial in early 1868. Unable or simply unwilling to continue some of Lincoln's policies after the war, Johnson managed to squander several important opportunities for reconstruction—or "restoration" as he preferred to call it.

Will and the electorate hoped that Grant's demonstrated skill on the battlefield would assist his ability to handle national affairs in the White House. His inauguration proved to be a highly anticipated affair and by March 1, crowds began descending on Washington D.C. for the festivities. There had been few times in recent memory when the Capitol had reason to celebrate. For the last nine years it had usually been either reeling from casualty figures of the war or draped in mourning for a fallen president. Red, blue, and white bunting festooned government offices leading to the White House; carriages whizzed up and down Pennsylvania Avenue to the strains of the "Commander's March." Dinner and cocktail parties filled out the social calendar, culminating in the inaugural ball held the night of Grant taking the oath of office. "Will you grant me the pleasure," Will asked Queen, "of escorting you to the inaugural ball?"

After standing through a cold drizzle at the inauguration, the couple joined a hundred or so high-ranking officers and ladies in toasting Mr. and Mrs. Grant in the Treasury Department ballroom. The men exchanged their ribbon-bedecked uniforms for black ties, white gloves, coats and tails; the ladies danced and socialized in tiaras and long ball gowns. Palmer knew many of the officers attending that evening, including the hard-drinking Grant. It was perhaps the greatest collection of Union colonels, generals, and Civil War heroes in one room at one time.[3]

As the season wore on, the couple encountered all the joys and uncertainties of new love. Queen asked if it was all right for her to call him Will. The general affectionately called her Queenie. He dropped off his calling card, asking her for a carriage ride in the park. They went to the opera, read the same books, enjoyed the same paintings, and gradually shared both their insecurities and fears. They were particularly fond of Romanticism in all its forms—painting, music, and in the literature of the time. They frequently traded their favorite sequences from stories they were reading, in once case *Undine and Lintram*, a tale from German folklore popular among Victorian readers. Queen became accustomed to Will's absences—usually for some business reason—but in the next moment they could irritate her as well.

While Queen usually remained at the family's home in Flushing, vagabond Will traveled around the country creating a network of acquaintances and business prospects. When Will was in New York, he often invited Queen to a gathering of friends or to an important lecture, one entitled "Sherman's March to the Sea," delivered by the blustery Hugh Kilpatrick, a major general who often spoke on important Civil War battles. The year 1869 was a cardinal year in railroad travel: in May the transcontinental railroad was completed and later celebrated with the driving of a golden spike at Promontory Point, Utah. Although Palmer was not there for the event, he and everyone else felt the ripples of its accomplishment. By that year the development of railroad connections was increasing month by month. Queen often wrote him impassioned letters, professing her love and divulging her dreams for the future. Will, in turn, shared his infatuation with her and often his insecurities. On April 3, 1869, he wrote from Chicago:

> While lying in a sick bed this morning I had a serious thinking over. I do not believe much in confessions or promises of amendment until the result is achieved—I will simply state the conclusions I came to— and these briefly—1st. That the wickedest man in New York was nothing to me. 2. That I intend to be good—My life has been a chequered one, with all sorts of experiences among all sorts of people—I cannot say that it has been an unhappy one, because I have been too reckless to care for consequences, or the opinions of people ... But my creed has always been better than my practice—and hereafter I am determined that they shall be made nearer to square—not by lowering the former but by bringing up the latter—so that with your love I expect to attain, even in this life, a share of the positive happiness which is so different a thing from the absence of misery, or from stoicism.

A few weeks later, from Chicago, he wrote to her again:

> Do not hesitate, my darling, to tell me how much you love me. You cannot spoil me in that way. You would not fear if you knew what an

inspiration it is to me—and not only inspiration but a shield. Men in active life must have a thousand relations with people that they cannot anticipate or control. They are subjected to a wide variety of temptations in consequence—There is not time to sit down and deliberately assume the position that would maintain towards such and such a person or set of persons with whom the ever-shifting drama of life may throw you into relations that cannot be escaped. Even if there were time, changes that cannot be anticipated may render the course wrong which otherwise would have been right. How shall one who scarcely can count on spending a single week in any fixed place or among the same influences steer properly through this troubled tide?[4]

As their relationship deepened, Queen often fantasized where the couple might live. She thought New York City would do nicely. Palmer even floated the idea to Queen that he could direct operations from the East Coast. "You will be glad to learn," he noted, "that I have been made a director of the company. There is a disposition on the board to give me pretty much my choice of positions, either at New York to take charge of the financial operations of the company, or out West to manage the construction of the road. Which do you think best, my talented business partner?"[5] If Will chose New York, Queen envisioned that he would have a spacious office, perhaps overlooking Franklin Square. She would arrange their social events and prepare her trained mezzo voice for an evening's entertainment in the couple's upscale, not too pretentious, Manhattan or Long Island home. Only by the summer of 1869 did this dream begin to crumble.

It was at this time that the relationship passed its first hurdle. Either directly or indirectly, Queen had conveyed to General Palmer that she was not part of his regiment, and therefore did not march to his orders. The often-authoritarian general had to use more subtle powers of persuasion, and Palmer came to admire and respect her insistent, independent nature.

From Chicago, St. Louis, Denver, and Philadelphia letters and telegrams arrived at the Mellen home on Long Island. Some were brief, telling Queen that he was safe and was thinking of her. Others from Will were longer and more intimate. In response, Queen penned by candlelight: "Only one page tonight to tell you that I am well and that I love you with all my heart—it is late—and I'm very, very tired—God bless my Will—my prayers are all yours—my soul itself lives but for you—dear love. Good night—your own little girl."[6]

In July one of his surveys took Will south of Denver along the Front Range of the Rockies. In an area below what is now the Palmer Divide, he discovered the land of his youthful visions. At an elevation that varied between 6,000 and 7,000 feet above sea level, the landscape lay below the base of Pikes Peak, dotted here and there by great swaths of dark pine and punctuated by large meadows of light green prairie grass and tufts of Spanish bayonet. To the west, the mountains towered over the scene, and near their slopes alabaster and salmon-colored rock formations rose in slender fingers to the sun. The air was sharp and elastic. On a clear day he could see the Spanish Peaks, pale and distant, to the south. It was a land that could make a man dream and bring his wife. Palmer dreamed. On July 28 he wrote Queen:

> After another day and night from Pueblo I reached here at 10 p.m. yesterday.
>
> For 120 miles from the Arkansas River we rode along the base, and generally within full view of the Rocky Mountains. These grand old mountains—how natural they seem and what a treat it always is to come back to them. The night ride was by moonlight. I spread out my blankets on top of the coach ... and slept soundly in the fresh air, until wakened by the round moon looking steadily into my face when I found the magnificent Pikes Peak towering immediately above at the elevations of over 14,000 ft., topped with a little snow. I could not sleep any more with all the splendid panorama of mountains gradually unrolling itself, as the moon faded and the sun began to rise, but sleepy though I was, I sat up and drank in, along with the purest mountain air, the full exhilaration of that early morning ride ...
>
> Near here are the finest springs of soda—and the most enticing scenery. I am sure there will be a famous resort here soon after the RRD reaches Denver. The scenery is even finer south of Denver than north of it, and besides the grass is greener, there is more water, a little forest of pine occasionally, and the sight is gladdened by the rude but

comfortable farm houses, which are dotted almost continuously from the Arkansas to the Platte. If I go back the same way I shall try to stop at the Garden of the Gods and run up to the summit of Ute Pass to take a look over into South Park ... I somehow fancied that an exploration of the dancing little tributaries ... might disclose somewhere up near to where they come leaping with delight from the cavernous wall of the Rocky Mountains, perhaps some charming spot which might be made a future home."

Palmer considered a north- south railroad linking Denver and Pueblo would come near—but not too near—the scenic area below Pikes Peak.

As Palmer poured out his visions for their future in his letters, she realized that her dream of living in the East was futile. She began imagining herself in the role of a western bride. Palmer was clear on the guidelines of his proposed Colorado utopia. He imagined a western resort similar to Newport, Rhode Island, or Saratoga Springs, New York, erected at the base of Pikes Peak. Alcohol drinkers need not arrive. Neither should penniless drifters or "fallen women." The town would cater to genteel easterners and Europeans who could afford a hundred dollar land certificate and were of good moral character. Schools and a college would follow; literature, science, and the arts would flourish. It would have wide, tree-lined streets on which fashionable shops, adequate bathhouses, and fine restaurants would do a brisk trade. There would be no labor strikes "against capitalists," he noted, "because they would all be capitalists in their way." He tried to assure her that they would not be too isolated: "Nor would we be without society when we wished for it. For sharing in the grand estate should be the homes of our friends—those really our friends. No fear but they would join us, for they would find nothing more attractive perhaps in the whole range of the Rocky Mountains. And they would be glad to make their summer home here also, here, where the air is fraught with health and vigour, and where life would be poetry ..."[7] By late July, Palmer was sold on the idea of living at the foot of Pikes Peak. That a man of the frontier could find his paradise out west—the still lawless West—was perfectly understandable, but liking a place and living there were two very different things, and so he worked extra hard at selling Queen on the idea and allaying her fears along the way. His prospective railroad was an important step in the process:

> I thought how fine it would be to have a little railroad a few hundred miles in length, all under one's control with one's friends, to have no jealousies and contests and differing policies, but to be able to carry out unimpeded and harmoniously one's views in regard to what ought and ought not to be done. In this ideal railroad all my friends should be interested, the most fitting men should be chosen for the different positions, and all would work heartedly and unitedly towards the common end ... Then I would have a nice house car made, just convenient for you and me, with perhaps a telegraph operator and a secretary, to travel up and down when business demanded, and this car should contain every convenience of lounging while in motion: but everything should go along smoothly that it would not be necessary to devote a very large proportion of the time to business.[8]

Utopias, railroads, dream houses—all very well, but first the area had to be, if not subdued, at least accustomed to. The eastern slopes of the Rockies had their unique set of weather problems, many of which Palmer would only experience much later. Violent thunderstorms bearing large hailstones shredded leaves and crops; windstorms roared down the canyons and blew trains off their tracks; late season storms, sometimes in May, piled up snow shoulder deep; tornadoes, although infrequent, threatened settlers. But these were minor inconveniences in comparison to what the land afforded.

The region was not completely uninhabited. A few ranches and cabins were scattered along what is now Templeton Gap. The remnants of Colorado City, just south of the Garden of the Gods, remained after the gold strike of 1859: a grim collection of storefronts and houses strewn up the mouth to Ute Pass. But for the most part, the major commercial routes bypassed the Front Range, endeavoring to cross the continent by way of New Mexico or Wyoming.

Indians were a concern on the eastern plains. Bands of Sioux,

Cheyenne, and Arapahoe roamed the prairies following the herds of buffalo. They rarely attacked large settlements. Railroad gangs, however, were frequent targets. Even with cavalry escort out of Fort Wallace, survey, grading, and track laying gangs were harassed and murdered by marauding Indians, such as the incident on May 13, 1870, when Cheyenne warriors killed twelve of Palmer's men in eastern Colorado. The following day he reported: "The fighting along our line in the Big Sandy Valley continued today. A large body of Indians, nearly 200, attacked a train four miles east of Lake, killing four and wounding one. Our grading has stopped between River Head and Kit Carson, and I fear our tie teams which we have gathered from the uttermost parts of New Mexico and Colorado with so many pains will be scattered to the four winds again."[9]

The Indians hated and feared the iron horse. Early in the decade, Sioux and Arapahoe braves tried to ensnare the snorting monster by stringing rawhide at eye level across the track as the engine neared. When that failed, they shot arrows and fired at it with repeating rifles stolen from government agents. They even tried lassoing it, but to no avail. The only prevention was to try and forestall the opening of their lands by killing railroad crews. Palmer often rode his horse named Don out to the track-laying gangs to monitor operations. Wearing a wide-brimmed dark hat and sitting gracefully astride his mount, he supervised the track heading through the towns of Kit Carson and Cheyenne Wells. "Do not have any apprehensions for my safety," he assured Queen. "The Indians are not desirous of butting heads against an organized body of mounted men and it's not like fighting rebels. We all think if the savages get one good vigorous lesson now they will stop giving us trouble until the road is completed; otherwise there will be constant danger." He worried about Queen coming west under such circumstances. "It makes me tremble," he wrote, "when I think of the risk."[10]

In early 1870, Palmer was writing to Queen: "Could we ever live away from the mountains? Perhaps so, but I think it would always feel like exile to both of us, and that home would always feel as if it was embalmed in the shade of these grand old peaks. I feel all my former enthusiasm coming back on reaching this mountain base, which seems, after crossing the plains, like the shore of a glorious new land."[11] Such dreams to pour into his lover's heart! But Palmer knew he needed to act to secure the land for himself, his future bride, and for the type of city he wanted to create. He began buying parcels of land surrounding the point where Fountain Creek intersected Monument Creek. He was especially attracted to a canyon just north of Garden of the Gods that he called Bijou (jewel). He wrote Queen on February 7: "Governor Hunt has undertaken to have Bijou surveyed and secured for me, so it can be safe for you to come out ... I told you about the beautiful secluded park that would make such a fine spot for a well to do colony of forty families. I have called it Queen's Park, after a certain royal creature."[12] The canyon and the home site, later called Glen Eyrie, haunted the general's thoughts for the next few months. Would Queen like it? Could she surrender her New York culture and live here amid Palmer's mountains?

Hope and doubt warred with each other for several months. Palmer arranged for Queen and her father to travel to the new colony and see her prospective future home. But before he asked her West, he proposed marriage in the parlor of the Mellen's Long Island home.

Although railroad companies touted the railroad as the most comfortable and fastest way to see the continent, some passengers of the early 1870s likened it to riding a buckboard over a corduroy road. The hard wooden seats were a problem. The aisles were crammed with immigrants heading west. Indian attacks, although infrequent, continued to make passengers wary of the horizon. But for many travelers it surpassed the other modes of travel, such as the stagecoach, which might take someone six days to travel from St. Louis to Denver.

For Queen Mellen, now twenty and engaged to be married to General Palmer, it was a grand adventure to see Will's paradise at Pikes Peak. Her father, William Mellen, accompanying her on the westbound train through Kansas, reminded her that the West was a dangerous place but that he would take care of her. As the waist-high prairie grasses gave way to the ankle-high stubble of eastern Colorado, Queen could look out the window and the see the vague profile of Pikes Peak far in the distance. The train deposited them at the railroad head at Kit Carson, a drab outpost on the treeless plains.

Even her most sordid daydreams could not prepare her for the misery of her surroundings, and it was still another fifty miles to Pikes Peak. Snow was falling lightly, accompanied by a bitter north wind, a combination that was sure to echo and enlarge the emptiness of any traveler's heart. The surrounding plains rose and faded into a white emptiness.

It was mid-April 1870. Back in Long Island daffodils were blooming in people's yards. Robins were pulling worms from green lawns. But here in eastern Colorado—Will's Colorado—it looked like upstate New York in December. Will had arranged for a coach to carry Queen and her father the remaining distance to the new colony. They jostled along through a thin layer of snow and across lakebeds of dry alkali, finally arriving in Will's presence the following day.

The weather was no better in the cold shadow of Pikes Peak. A brisk wind carried a sprinkling of snow showers throughout the day; the great mountain and the Front Range were shrouded in mist. Civilization was absent. The dun-colored grasses stretched to the base of the foothills rising into the clouds. Her mood improved when Palmer whisked her and her father out over the mesa to Queen's Canyon where Will had picked their home site.

At that point Queen had every opportunity to turn around, head back East, and confess to Will that this was no land for her. But as if summoning some pioneer spirit deep inside her, she stayed. She not only stayed, but she began making plans for their life together here. Amid the raw April weather, the canyon was beautiful: dotted with pines and Douglas fir, it wound up the mountain through many twists and turns. Huge rock spurs were home to blue jays and hawks. She named their home site Glen Eyrie because it was home to several eagles' nests.

She drew up some rough plans for their new house, envisioning hexagonal rooms surrounding a huge central chimney. The first floor was reserved for Queen and Will. It had tall spacious windows admitting three hundred days of sunshine a year. The second floor had a boy's room, girl's room, teacher's room, and a larger schoolroom. The third floor was set aside for servants' quarters and a storage or "trunk" room. The basement held a wine cellar—even though the general did not drink—and coal and wood storage.

The weather and the surroundings were not the only things to test Queen's mettle. An unthinking local settler pointed out the spot where two boys had been murdered by Indians the year before. Added to the tales of warring Indians in the region, the news unsettled Queen. Her uncle, Malcolm Clark, had been killed by Indians in Montana some time before, so she remained on edge about the Indian peril.

With mixed feelings, she and her father left Colorado and headed back to New York, leaving Will to use his tender lash and savvy business skills in turning this prairie homestead into the city that would become Colorado Springs. More lots had to be purchased as well, most at about $1.25 per acre, as plans for platting the town continued. He employed the El Paso County clerk, Irving Howbert, to oversee the legal aspects of development. He pushed through plans to run his north- south railroad from Denver to Pueblo, with a whistle stop in Colorado Springs. Palmer envisioned a fine gray stone depot befitting the high quality of life in the new city. In October 1870, Will's Front Range railroad was named the Denver and Rio Grande and began limited service. It inaugurated a host of interlocking enterprises—cities, coal mines, and other infrastructure—that would civilize the Colorado territory and make Palmer one of its most famous, and richest, citizens.[13] Statehood for Colorado was still six years away, but Palmer seemed bent on making his mark on the region as soon as possible.

Will was not totally inconsiderate about Queen's misgivings in living in the new territory. He believed, maybe more in his lover's heart than in his head, that she would grow to love it. In the meantime, he played up the quality of the air, the opportunity for decent and affluent citizens to enjoy the mountains free of some of the hardscrabble conditions of other frontier towns. He wrote a stream of letters to Queen encouraging these ideas as well as predicting her future role in the education of its children and the direction of the town's social life. "You will have plenty to do, will you not, in looking after all these colonies. I don't know who will be busiest, you or I?"[14]

By 1870, the population of Flushing, Long Island, was approaching 35,000. It attracted affluent professionals working in New York who could not afford Manhattan. William Proctor Mellen and his family were part of this particular group who settled in an attractive part of Flushing. While the outer fringes of the city were ethnically homogenous, the downtown business district was soon sporting signs in Russian, German, Polish, and Norwegian. The influx of immigrants in central New York was beginning to spill out into the suburbs and soon Flushing began to feel the swell of overcrowding.

On the other hand, nearby New York City was, well, New York City—noisy, crowded, and pulsing with energy. The gilt of the Gilded Age was beginning to adorn its halls, buildings, and brownstones. The wealthy such as the Vanderbilts, Astors, and Roosevelts gathered along Broadway and Fifth Avenue, while the less fortunate and immigrants started pouring into places like Hell's Kitchen and Five Points. Although the advent of the skyscraper was years away, the shapes of industrial growth and a burgeoning economy started rising into the air. Private mansions, as the new symbols of wealth, started springing up throughout the heart of the city.

When William Jackson Palmer arrived in New York in early November, he witnessed what the right amount of money could buy. One of his friends was John Taylor Johnston, president of the New Jersey Railroad, who had recently been elected the first president of the Metropolitan Museum of Art. Johnston was affluent enough to build the first marble home in New York, at Number 8 Fifth Avenue. Although he was more than fifteen years older than Palmer, he shared a memory with the general. Five years before, in 1865, he had toured the prison at Castle Thunder in Richmond, Virginia—the same jail where Palmer had languished for four months during the war. Witnessing what Palmer had endured created a bond between the two men. Johnston thought Palmer a great American hero, and did his best to finance and further the general's ambitions in building a network of railroads. Palmer was entranced by Johnston's marble mansion. Peering out through the windows at the tall wrought iron gates, neat lawns, and the four-in-hands clopping along Fifth Avenue, William could dream of his own castle at Glen Eyrie.

On November 8, 1870, the couple was married in the Mellen home. Queen wore a white satin dress and had her hair pulled back in a bun. In addition to William and Ellen Mellen, all her half-siblings were in attendance. The idea that Will Palmer was building something fantastic out West—what, they did not know—increased their excitement.

The couple left the following day for Europe, sailing aboard the RMS *Scotia*, a Cunard paddle steamer much favored by the Roosevelts for travel abroad and one that set the Atlantic crossing speed record some years before. On the voyage, Queen began keeping a honeymoon journal in which she noted passenger names and residences, conversations, cryptic initials, and other scribbles that might jog her memory later. The first class accommodations were opulent for the time, featuring padded satin chairs, brass lamps with shades fringed in gold tassels, and white chintz curtains. With impeccable service, the days sped by until landing in Liverpool a short time later.

It did not seem to matter to Will that Europe was in turmoil due to the Franco-Prussian War occurring at the time. The last thing the Continent needed was some bubbly American newlyweds hobnobbing around the country while a war in France was going on. But Great Britain so far was stable, as were the Netherlands and Belgium. Will and Queen hoped to stay with English friends, and Will in particular wished to see how the British had advanced the railroads since his visit back in 1855.

Their three-month honeymoon in Europe began the morning of the twentieth of November when they arrived at the Liverpool docks and were greeted by Dr. Willie Bell, Palmer's aide on his trek west. Joining them was Bell's sister, Ettie, who quickly became friends with Queen. Bell served as an important contact in England by introducing the Palmers to several notable families during their stay. After lunching at the Adelphi Hotel, they left by train for London. For a few days they stayed at the "comfortable but not elegant" Buckingham Palace Hotel directly across from Queen Victoria's residence.[15] Queen was delighted the Union Jack was flying over the palace, signifying that the monarch was indeed staying there.

The next few days were filled with sightseeing opportunities from the Houses of Parliament to Westminster Abbey and Hall. In the afternoon they shopped on Bond and Regent Streets; at night they attended the opera or a concert. While Will sought out business prospects to help finance his railroad to Mexico, Queen and Mrs. Bell took the tube to Madam Tussaud's Wax Museum. By the end of November, the Bells invited them to stay at their home in the city, where they regaled the newlyweds with dinner parties and amateur, impromptu musical concerts. Possessed of a beautiful, disciplined singing voice, Queen was often called upon to entertain the group. Their English acquaintances were eager to hear about the couple's tales of the Wild West, particularly about those involving Indians and the cavalry. At such times, William modestly spoke of his service in the war and of his exploits in Arizona and California. On some evenings, Will left alone to meet a businessman while Queen stayed by herself in the Bell's flat, writing letters and reading Dickens and Thackeray.

One of Will's most significant trips out of London proved to be to the Ffestiniog Railway in Wales, one of the first successful narrow gauge trains in Great Britain. The line was constructed between 1833 and 1836 to carry slate from the Welsh mountains to the port of Porthmadog on the coast. The company's success was further evidence for Will that a narrow gauge would be ideal in the Colorado mountain passes. Standard gauge rails were four feet, eight and one-half inches wide, but the narrow gauge ranged from two feet wide in certain terrain to three feet wide in others. Based on his observations, Will ordered narrow gauge rails to be shipped directly from Wales to Colorado.

Queen's generous and compassionate spirit was on full display that Christmas season. As London was the largest city in Europe, it was also noted for its widespread poverty. One day she and Ettie walked down to the East End and found "a poor child to make warm.

I found one boy for whom I got a strong pair of boots and stockings and a little girl whom I made very comfortable with a knit woolen jacket, tippet stockings, gloves, etc."[16]

By extending her goodwill to the strangers and dispossessed of London, Queen opened up a new chapter in her life, a chapter that she was not even probably aware of at the time. With its spacious city parks and bridges, theater and opera houses, London and then its environs were to become her second home. Although she did not rave in her journal, she took immediately to its history and culture. She loved its gentility and manners, qualities she found particularly lacking west of St. Louis. Outside of London, the serene countryside, even in the grayness of winter, spoke to her gentle nature. She felt warm and secure in England, perhaps more so than she did at any other place in her short life.

The English, too, opened their hearts to her and Will. After visiting Amsterdam and Brussels, they were invited (through Willie Bell) to the country home of Charles Kinglsey, who by most people's standards of the day was in a league with Dickens, Carlyle, Tennyson, George Eliot, and John Ruskin. A prolific writer of over forty books, including the famous *Westward Ho!* and *Water Babies*, and a former Cambridge University Professor of Modern History, Kingsley was also a well-known cleric in the Church of England. He became acquainted with the Palmers during his service as rector of Eversley in Hampshire. He and his wife, Fanny, had three children: Rose, Maurice, and Mary. Tall, dark-haired, and lanky with dark mutton chop side whiskers, the gracious Kingsley invited many guests of all backgrounds and beliefs to his country home in Hampshire.

When the Palmers arrived in February, a fire crackled in the central fireplace. Mr. Kingsley met them at the door and led them into the parlor where Rose and Fanny awaited them. The Palmers were generally courteous guests, but Queen could be picky with her meals, preferring "bacon for breakfast—fried thin," and "coppery oysters—not broiled."[17]

Over several days they traded stories of their native lands. Since Charles's son Maurice, aged twenty-three, had expressed interest in visiting and working in America, Will offered him to be part of his new enterprise in Colorado. The twenty-five-year-old Rose, gregarious, restless, and adventuresome, also expressed interest in visiting the West.

The Kingsley home, the Rectory, a three-story historical but modest country home, was also of interest to the Palmers. Strolling one day in the garden, the Palmers considered the Rectory a perfect model for their future home. Although the home was not strictly Gothic—mainly English Tudor—it seemed stately and cozy enough for the visiting couple. Despite several modifications and changes over the years, Charles Kingsley's home became the prototype of Will and Queen's dream home at Glen Eyrie.

On February 11, 1871, the day before they were to sail for America, Queen's honeymoon journal abruptly ends. The next page is torn from the binding. What had happened? Had the couple quarreled? Had Will's business meetings dampened their honeymoon joy? Did some of Queen's notations seem too frivolous for the moment and therefore unnecessary? We can only conjecture. Queen's journal does not resume for four years and several tragedies later.

After the Palmers arrived in New York, Will left Queen at the Mellen home while he headed West to resume the building of his Colorado resort. Will could call it a western Newport, Saratoga Springs, Babylon, Utopia, or whatever he liked, but others saw it for what it was: a strip of dirt with twelve squat and irregular half-finished buildings.

Upon arriving in Denver, Will plunged into the creation of his new town. He knew that it was critical to link the town site with the arrival of the railroad. Hence, the town and railroad were simultaneously developed. Track was laid in the spring and summer of 1871 from Denver to the depot below Pikes Peak. Two of his regimental friends from Pennsylvania, Major Henry McAlister and Colonel W.H. Greenwood, directed the rail operation between Denver and Pikes Peak. On July 26, the first Denver and Rio Grande locomotive, the Montezuma, arrived in Denver from Philadelphia, later to begin service to the newly created Fountain Colony—eventually known as Colorado Springs.

Palmer formed the Colorado Springs Company to supervise the creation and construction of his town site. By late July the company was pleased to announce that it had platted one thousand acres of lots with unusually wide streets, sufficient parks, gardens, and squares running east of Monument Creek and two miles from north to south.[18] On July 31, 1871, the town of Colorado Springs, still a cluster of creosote-stained boards with a creek snaking through it, was ready for the first stake ceremony. In front of an assembled crowd, the town manager, General Cameron, mounted a platform and boasted of the town's potential: "This favored spot, sheltered by the divide from the storms of the north, is soon to blossom into gardens of beauty and houses where elegance reigns; here will rise groves and orchards and over these hills the luxuriant vine will climb and yield its fruit in its season."[19] Maurice Kingsley had traveled from Hampshire to become Palmer's secretary treasurer of the Colorado Springs Company and represented the business at the festivities.

While the fledgling town enjoyed its shining moment, Will was kept busy advising Queen of the progress of their Glen Eyrie home. On July 7 he bravely asked her if her father could "go to the government second-hand store ... to obtain some tents to use until the house is completed. It would be pleasanter and cheaper than hotel life, even if the hotel is completed in time, which is doubtful, and we would be right on the ground during completion to decide details of finishing, which is exceedingly important." His suggestion at first must have made Queen shudder. Tents, second-hand stores, indeed. The following day he tried to smooth things over: "What happy days we shall spend here planning and working to improve our lovely home."[20]

The home he was planning was far from the baronial mansion he initially had in mind. For one thing he could not afford it. Secondly, the labor and materials were not available for such a venture. He settled for a gabled, three-story, fourteen-room house, nestled on the gentle slope of the canyon with an attractive view of the glen.

On the tenth of July he penned: "The Glen, our Glen has many

Surveying the streets for Colorado Springs, circa 1871-72. Palmer wearing hat in center. Courtesy of the Starsmore Center for Local History, Colorado Springs Pioneers Museum.

wild raspberries in it now." High summer in Queen's Canyon provided not only wild raspberries, but Virginia creeper, clematis, Indian paintbrush, sego lily, and carpets of green buffalo grass kept lush by constant afternoon rains. As construction of the house was occurring, big horn sheep and elk often roamed deep into the canyon.

Glen Eyrie lay about three miles as the crow flies from the center of Colorado Springs. Five ecosystems were located on the property: grassland, riparian, mountain-shrub, juniper, and pine and Douglas fir forest. Tangles of low-growing scrub oak and willows bordered the valley. Rattlesnakes and lizards were common but Will had ordered some pigs to be turned loose to abate any danger. Other writers found it "a strange wild savage place and yet beautiful—green and fresh when all without is bare and brown," wrote Grace Greenwood in 1873. Just south of the property lay the Garden of the Gods, described by writer Helen Hunt Jackson as a "supernatural catastrophe."[21]

Palmer often rode his horse between the glen and the town center.

He returned at night to bed down under the bough of a Douglas fir tree and watched his kingdom soften into darkness. He took pleasure in claiming the region as his and Queen's. In a letter he insisted that she begin naming the unique rock formations in the glen. Eventually she came up with an eclectic list that reflected her journeys and interests. The shape guarding the valley was dubbed Major Domo. From that decision came other names such as King Arthur's Seat, Punchinello, Abraham Lincoln, and Montezuma. A serrated file of rocks was dubbed Echo Rocks.

Palmer, Queen, and the town manager, General Cameron, soon provided the names of the city streets, which included Cucharras, Vermijo, Costilla, Cascade, Boulder, and St. Vrain. Some streets were named for nearby mountain ranges, others for streams and rivers in Colorado and the Rockies. Palmer himself named one the town's major arteries, Pikes Peak Avenue, which was laid out extra wide to accommodate people, wagons, and carriages.

By September and his thirty-fifth birthday, Will was sufficiently panic stricken over Queen's imminent arrival. But there were complications. The house would not be finished until the first part of the new year. They would have to get by in tents and other makeshift structures as time went along. News reached Palmer that the entire Mellen family—consisting of William, Ellen, and their six children— would be settling in the new town. They also would need a place to stay, and Will suggested that it would be with the Palmers. In the meantime, they would need a roof over their heads through the fall and winter. The general was also advised that Rose Kingsley, Charles Kingsley's daughter, would be arriving in early November to help Queen get settled.

In town, other plans were evolving. Thousands of cottonwood trees were planted to provide shade and beautify the landscape. More permanent structures were replacing the ramshackle buildings in the center of the city. A three-story hotel was in the works, to be completed by the first days of the new year. Newly arrived settlers had begun erecting houses along the main streets and within a short time they extended in the four directions around Fountain Creek. It was evident that the general's vision for the place was taking tangible shape.

Queen of Hearts

When Queen and the Mellen family arrived by train in late October, Will Palmer made the unpardonable mistake of not being there for the occasion. It was an error in judgment more concerning emotional intimacy than etiquette that would haunt the Palmer marriage for the first few years and into the next decade. Will, often too distracted by business, missed the important occasions that Queen Palmer craved. The general thought he was acting in the couple's best interest by attending affairs away from home. But Queen thought otherwise. Will's inadvertent missing of a birthday or a special occasion hurt Queen more than he knew. He could place his guilt elsewhere or blame it on outside events, but the point was he missed the minor moments of the heart that bond lovers together.

While Queen was arriving in Colorado Springs, Will was scrambling over a craggy rock face in the Arkansas River canyon in southern Colorado, hoping to survey a route through the heart of the Royal Gorge. He discovered some of the most ruggedly beautiful country in the Rockies. He knew that a route through the central

A treeless Pikes Peak Avenue in 1875. Courtesy of the Starsmore Center for Local History, Colorado Springs Pioneers Museum.

Rockies would open up productive lands on the Western Slope and in Utah. The Denver and Rio Grande Railroad was in a position to secure the right of way through the mountains by way of the Grand Canyon of the Royal Gorge, a difficult, and at the time, a near-impossible project. When the right of way was made part of the charter of the Denver and Rio Grande, Palmer could move forward with mapping, surveying, and staking the route.

In Colorado Springs, Dr. Bell greeted Queen and the Mellens and whisked them up to his log cabin in nearby Manitou. For the first several days, Queen and the Mellens stayed in tents, but as winter crept along they moved into the barn behind the Palmer's uncompleted house in the glen. Even the hardiest greenhorn would have been traumatized by the geographical and cultural shift, but for Queen, celebrating her first wedding anniversary without her husband, it was additionally disheartening. A few days later a letter arrived from Will: "I think you must be in Colorado by now ... I hope you have not over-exerted yourself in the bustle of moving and that when I reach our tent home in Glen Eyrie I will find you in the best of health."[1] By this time they had moved out of the tents and into a wooden shelter euphemistically called the Manitou Hotel.

Arriving on the first of November for a four-month sojourn, the intrepid Rose Kingsley helped Queen make the transition from an eastern sophisticate to a Colorado pioneer. She and Queen were both young and spirited enough to turn what could have been a marital disaster into a pleasant adventure. Even after the general returned, Rose was able to assist Queen and the Mellens in getting settled in the new land. She joined her brother Maurice, who was busy keeping current the financial accounts of the Colorado Springs Company.

Like many of the new arrivals, Rose tempered her lofty expectations with the harsh realities of the region. She recorded her experiences in her insightful book, *South by West*, of 1874:

> You may imagine Colorado Springs, as I did, to be a sequestered valley, with bubbling fountains, green grass, and shady trees; but not a bit of it. Picture to yourself a level elevated plateau of greenish-brown, without a single tree or plant larger than a Spanish bayonet two feet high, sloping down a quarter of a mile to the railroad track and Monument Creek, and you have a pretty good idea of the town site as it appears in November 1871.
>
> The street and blocks are only marked out by a furrow turned with a plough, and indicated faintly by a wooden house, finished, or in the process of building, here and there, scattered over half a mile of prairie. About twelve houses and shanties are inhabited, most of them being unfinished, or run up for temporary occupation; and there are several tents dotted about also.[2]

Rose soon settled into a sixteen by twelve foot shanty thrown together in two days by Maurice. Her brother attached his tent to the front door so that they could use it as a sitting room during the day. On the floor they threw down a buffalo rug and draped a red California blanket over their wall. A little stove in the corner served as warmth on the frigid winter nights. "I locked myself into my strange abode, and with M's revolver as protection against imaginary foes; and by dint of buffalo-robes and blankets, and heaps of flannel, managed to keep tolerably warm, though my breath condensed on the sheets, and when I got up the bucket had a quarter inch of ice on it."[3]

Garbed in tweeds and wearing a stout pair of walking shoes, Rose tramped about the town and through the surrounding foothills. The strange land with its evergreens and rust-colored earth entranced her. When she was not freezing in her shack or washing clothes in a bucket, she thrilled at the arrival of the Santa Fe stage and the thunderous engine of the Denver and Rio Grande pulling in from

Glen Eyrie and Queen's Canyon looking west taken from the mesa circa 1900. Courtesy of the Starsmore Center for Local History, Colorado Springs Pioneers Museum.

Denver. Outside her house, hammering and sawing—the audible moments of a city rising from the ground—continued through the morning, afternoon, and into dusk. Invited to various homes, she enjoyed evening courses of venison, baked potatoes, and blackberry preserves on bread, and washed down by black coffee served on English bone china. She witnessed the painstaking job of constructing the Palmer's Glen Eyrie house during late autumn and into winter. Work was frequently interrupted by fierce November and December winter squalls followed by periods of warm sunshine.

In mid-November Queen began teaching school for five or six children at a temporary location on Cascade Avenue. She packed her saddlebags full of books, mounted her horse, and rode into town, where she was often prevented from lecturing by one or two unruly kids who took to throwing paper wads at the girls. The *Rocky Mountain News* ran a story the following morning congratulating Queen on her altruism. "The motive that prompted a wealthy, refined, and educated lady to inaugurate and personally superintend this primitive educational institution is, to say the least, a worthy example of Christian charity as we deem highly commendable."[4] She endured a short spell of teaching, then turned her duties over to Rose as she left town for some rest.

On Thanksgiving Day Queen and Will traveled by train to Denver where they had dinner with Major General William Rosecrans, who had fought with Palmer during the Battle of Chattanooga and was the former U.S. Ambassador to Mexico. Being familiar with the countryside and with a wide circle of friends in Mexico, Rosecrans served to educate Palmer about the possibilities of a railroad route from Colorado to Mexico City. After their encounter in Denver, Will once again became restless and began planning his own trip to Mexico for the following spring to finally make his idea a reality.

The future seemed suddenly very bright for the Palmers. The Denver and Rio Grande, which Queen reminded him was "hers too," continued to turn profits weekly. The city they had founded was attracting new settlers. The house they had designed in "their glen" was well underway to being completed. For Will, the bird of inspiration had hardly enough time to alight before taking off in a new direction.

The winter of 1871–72 came in with a fury, shutting down the rails on the eastern plains and piling up three-foot high snowdrifts in the Pinery (now the Black Forest) north of town. The antelope huddled along a ridge of the forest waiting for the sun. When the trains finally arrived a few days late, Rose reported, "the wheels and every ledge and corner were a mass of snow, and the icicles hung in a crystal fringe all over the boiler." She also concluded that the "narrow gauge holds its own against the broad gauge, and a freight train got through behind the passenger cars yesterday." While the railroads remained snarled because the storm, "the sleigh owners made small fortunes by eight to ten dollars an hour."[5]

But Rose and Queen were surprised by how quickly the down-sloping winds, called chinooks by the Indians, could suddenly raise temperatures by thirty or forty degrees, melting the snow and allowing passage through the muddy thoroughfares. On such days they could ride up and explore the Garden of the Gods. As an extremely astute British writer, Kingsley could focus on things that a native reporter might overlook. Colorful rock formations in the garden, often resembling human and animal forms, particularly intrigued her. In *South by West* she reveled at the "many weird animal figures praying, with their heads all bent towards Cheyenne Mountain; then a red sandstone nun with a white cowl over her head, looking at a seal who stood on his tail and made faces at her ... the great rocks were a warm salmon colour, with green pines growing in their crevices, bringing out the richness of their colouring and between them as if set in a glowing frame shone Pikes Peak, covered in snow ..."[6]

As smoke from their fires trailed listlessly against the white snow and the leaden skies, Colorado Springs enjoyed its first Christmas. Although primitive, it was a joyous and festive affair. Pine boughs covered the entrances to shanties and buildings. Townspeople cut a ponderosa and erected it in Foote's Hall where twenty couples celebrated the season with a gala ball. Queen hosted a Christmas party for her pupils, ending the celebration with several Verdi arias.

The new year brought more exciting developments for the city. On January 1, 1872, the Colorado Springs Hotel opened its doors. Advertised by one citizen as "the most elegant hostelry between Chicago and San Francisco," it was a three-story, clapboard structure with a covered porch across the façade and could accommodate over sixty clients—roomed in close quarters if necessary.[7] On Charles Kingsley's recommendation, Mr. Elsom Tiller had arrived from England to become editor of Will Palmer's new magazine, Out West. Upset by the number of saloons in nearby Colorado City, Rose, Queen, and Maurice, but primarily Rose, began organizing a fundraising concert to finance a new library and reading room that would presumably counter the number of hard drinking dens springing up in the neighboring town.

Rose set the date of the concert for January 25. The town, which had reached a population of three hundred, housed in fifty-five cabins, eagerly attended the event held in Foote's Hall.

The weather turned miserably cold and windy, the temperature rarely reaching above zero degrees. During the practice session it dropped to nineteen degrees below zero. Between verses of the song, Rose had to jump and run over to the stove to thaw out her hands.[8]

The weather warmed the day of the concert to a few degrees above zero. Rose wore her rumpled tweeds that she never seemed to part with; Queen wore something more fashionable for her song numbers; Maurice wore a clean shirt and tie and a suit he had brought from England. By the start of the concert at eight p.m. over a hundred and fifty people crowded the hall, including several bull whackers who "had dropped in after their day's work with the ox and mule teams." The piano player hid a jug of eggnog under the piano so that performers could take a swig before heading onstage. Queen Palmer sang two or three popular ballads to "rapturous applause," noted Rose. Her brother crooned an old folk song: "When the fox went out on a moonlit night/prayed to the moon to give him light ..." The audience demanded two encores.[9]

"All went home delighted with their evening," said Rose. "The result to the reading room was most satisfactory, as after all expenses we netted sixty dollars, a creditable amount for a town only five months old."[10]

As the first winter wore on, more settlers and tourists began arriving. Some were fleeing the Chicago fire that had ravaged the city the previous October. Some were refugees leaving the cramped eastern cities. A few were foreign immigrants, such as the ones that arrived in February and confronted Maurice and Rose in the office of the Colorado Springs Company.

The family, consisting of a husband, wife, and three children from southern England, arrived expecting "a large town with fine farming lands, ploughed and fenced, all round," reported Rose. "They had neither bedding, nor any necessaries for life in a shanty." Rose and

Maurice put them up for the night in their own cabin. The Kingsleys and the Palmers had seen many before: new arrivals that had expected verdant fields, bubbling springs bordered by mossy glades, and extensive white fences. "They turn around and accuse those who have advised them to leave the struggle for existence in the old country, of sending them to their death and ruin in the new."[11] The Palmers heard reports of disgruntled settlers even trying to shoot the authors of the pamphlet that brought settlers west.

But for the most part, the city flourished. Those who came inevitably settled and worked the land or opened a trade shop. As the population swelled, available workers became scarce. One family requested that a girl come down from a ranch in the mountains to help with the cooking and cleaning. After staying less than a month, the girl left for Denver and another job because "the Springs was too dull for her."[12]

By the end of February and the beginning of March, the Palmer's house was ready for its occupants, although painters and trim

Glen Eyrie under construction early 1872. Courtesy of the Starsmore Center for Local History, Colorado Springs Pioneers Museum.

workers filtered in and out. The Palmers had been spending part of the winter above the stable in the barn, along with the Mellen family. The fifty-eight-year-old William and his thirty-five-year-old wife were expecting their seventh child.

The first version of the Glen Eyrie house was a humble structure compared to the later modifications and additions of 1881 and 1904 that produced the mansion that we know today.

However, this house was the nucleus of Palmer's vision for a grand, elegant structure befitting a thirty-five-year-old railroad magnate and his family. His stables were quickly filled with saddle horses and spirited Irish hunters. Long-eared and friendly hound dogs and later Great Danes had their run of the place.

As the plans for his Colorado to Mexico trip began shaping up, Will began to worry about Queen's health. She had experienced weakness in her limbs and dizzy spells for weeks. It may have been apparent to her that she was pregnant, but Queen did not use that reason to remain in Colorado while her husband journeyed to Mexico. On the contrary, she insisted that she accompany him, Rose, and Maurice to Mexico City. She was, in fact, a month into the pregnancy with her first child.

While a party of engineers headed overland to Mexico to rendezvous with the Palmers in Manzanillo, Mexico, the Palmers and Kingsleys took the train in early March to San Francisco, where they were joined by General Rosecrans. They soon boarded the packet *Alaska* bound for Manzanillo. Queen loved the refreshing Pacific breezes, especially after leaving some of the pioneering drudgeries of her chosen town. Although she loved the adventure of a new place, it had been a difficult and exhausting four months since she arrived. She hated the mud and grit of a frontier town, but she enjoyed being treated as royalty in a sequestered mountain hamlet. The townspeople, in turn, showered her with love and affection, often pausing to tip their hats at her carriage when she passed.

General Rosecrans, working independently, had secured permits from the Mexican government for Palmer to build one railroad from El Paso, Texas, to Mexico City and another from Mexico City to Manzanillo on the West Coast. Palmer and his party were expecting to obtain the final approval from the Mexican president before workers

Glen Eyrie, circa 1900, nestled among the trees planted by General Palmer. The Rampart Range is in the background. Courtesy of the Starsmore Center for Local History, Colorado Springs Pioneers Museum.

began laying tracks.

But Palmer and Rosecrans remained worried over the present state of turmoil in Mexico. The administration of President Juarez was under constant attack from insurrectionists and terrorist groups. Anti-Juarez guerilla bands harassed, robbed, and killed both travelers and villagers. As it turned out, Rosecrans and Palmer encountered great fortune on the ship when they met Porfirio Diaz, the tall, distinguished Mexican leader who opposed Juarez. Diaz was returning to Mexico to rally support for the ouster of Juarez and hopefully to get himself elected president. Palmer, the great opportunist, saw Diaz as an important segue into Mexican political power and hence to the formation of his railroad.

Palmer and Diaz talked throughout the voyage. The latter was quite enthusiastic about Palmer's vision for a Mexican railroad from the United States and assured the American that he would support such an enterprise once he was in power. Since Diaz was very influential throughout Mexico, he gave Palmer a coin with Diaz's name on it, which, presumably, would help Palmer travel safely through the countryside on his way to Mexico City.

During the passage across the Gulf of California, Palmer and Diaz also had a chance to teach Queen and Rose how to shoot Palmer's Colt army revolver. They chose floating debris for target practice, although Queen quickly lost interest after a few shots. Will knew that the route across the rugged mountains to Mexico City would be dangerous, so he prepared the young women as best as he could.

When they reached Manzanillo, they prepared for the 400-plus mile journey to the Mexican capital. By anyone's measure, it was a tough, dirty, and arduous trek. Diaz and his party left them at their first overnight stop. They traveled partly by mule caravan and then by stagecoach the rest of the way. Drowsy, ramshackle villages winked out through the haze of their centuries-long slumber. For the pregnant Mrs. Palmer it was particularly challenging. Often woozy and nauseous in the saddle, she did her best to keep going through squalid villages and across the rocky countryside. Rose and Maurice encouraged her throughout the journey. Travel by stagecoach was often as arduous as by mule or horseback. Coach drivers dashed through the hairpin turns and wildly drove their teams along the canyon rims.

After staying overnight at an inn in Cebolla, they encountered a band of Mexican rebels that galloped into town, firing their weapons in the air. The leader of the raffish band identified himself as a patriot who hated the dictator Benito Juarez. Looking over the strangers, the leader at first demanded all their possessions, including their clothing, weapons, and ammunition. General Palmer, who spoke some Spanish, persuaded the leader to reduce his demands to guns and ammunition.

Faced with little protection on the way to Mexico City, Palmer and Maurice cut tree branches with machetes and created durable clubs and staffs. Rose and Queen, sporting brave but frightened demeanors, soldiered on. When they arrived in Guadalajara, they were joined by the group of engineers that had traveled overland from Texas. The Palmer party bought new weapons and headed for the capital, which they reached on April 26, 1872.

The Mexican government had demanded price data from Palmer and Rosecrans on the proposed railroad. Therefore, Palmer, Rosecrans, and the engineers soon set off to scout and survey the route to the east coast of Mexico. Queen and Rose remained in Mexico City, resting in the mornings and sightseeing in the afternoons. After Will concluded his survey weeks later, he and his party returned to Mexico City to begin the negotiating process with the government. Will's diplomacy efforts fell on deaf ears. The Juarez regime was in no position to grant access for an American railroad to enter Mexico. After negotiations fell apart, Will decided to leave Rosecrans in Mexico to represent their interests and return to America.

Queen had insisted on having her baby in New York, so the Palmer group made their way to Veracruz on the Gulf of Mexico and then by ship to Havana and Cedar Key, Florida. They took the train to Richmond, Virginia, where Will had been imprisoned during the war, and continued on to New York where they arrived in mid-July. Maurice Kingsley, who had resigned as treasurer of the Colorado Springs Company, and sister Rose soon returned to England, having survived their lively introduction to the Wild West.

Will felt uneasy about his decision to leave his wife in New York to have her baby while he headed by train back to Colorado Springs. He continued to have mixed feelings after his arrival in mid-summer 1872, temporarily shelving his ambitions for a railroad in Mexico and focusing on the health of his city and the Denver and Rio Grande Railroad.

The period between 1870 and early 1873 saw staggering economic growth. The expansion of railroads led to an increasingly mobile population. As people continued moving West, city populations soared. Denver's increased from 5,000 to 18,000; Pueblo's from 500 to 4,000; and Colorado Springs' from 400 to 2,000. Colorado's population had jumped from 40,000 to well over a 100,000. As town sizes increased, land values in counties along the Front Range tripled in dollar value. Southern Colorado coal mines, in which Palmer began to invest heavily, were sending to market nearly 500 tons daily.

Will and Queen were swept along by this tide of wealth and prosperity. On October 30, 1872, Queen gave birth to Elsie Mellen Palmer in New York City. Will heard the news by telegraph in the offices of the Colorado Springs Company. Once assured that wife and baby were doing well, he left in December for Mexico City to resume his quest for a southern railroad. Those negotiations, too, collapsed.

By the spring of 1873, General Rosecrans had alienated most of his contacts in Mexico City. The Mexican Congress and President Juarez remained intractable. More fatigued by frustration than defeat, Palmer turned the light off his project, hoping that time and circumstance might once again revive his plans.

The arrival of Queen and baby Elsie lifted Will's spirits. Many Springs' residents turned out to welcome the two at the train depot. Queen's stepmother, Ellen, had recently given birth to a baby girl and although it felt socially awkward, Mrs. Palmer enjoyed raising their daughters together at Glen Eyrie.

Friendly, curious Ute Indians, who had lived peacefully in the area for centuries, sometimes wandered into the glen and peered through the Palmer's windows. The Indians and Queen often shared trinkets as diplomatic gestures. On one occasion an Indian man and his wife showed up at Glen Eyrie and asked if they could bathe their baby in the house nursery.[13]

The first five years after the city's founding produced a distinct new class of train passenger—the tourist—who trickled in at first, then arrived en masse. French tourists, German tourists, British tourists, along the lines of Rose Kingsley wearing tweeds and brogans, and a various assortment of Connecticut Yankees, New York Knickerbockers, and Boston blue bloods, arrived in Palmer's resort town to scale the mountains and imbibe the healing waters of Manitou. The general preferred to be on hand to greet them, but

The first Antlers Hotel circa 1885. Pikes Peak Avenue looking west with Pikes Peak in the background. Courtesy of the Starsmore Center for Local History, Colorado Springs Pioneers Museum.

as time went on he was increasingly away on railroad business. At 14,115 feet, Pikes Peak became a focal point of the town. People talked about it, venerated it, photographed and painted it, and even began hacking a trail up to its summit. Soon there were halfway and three-quarter way shelters for eager mountaineers as they trekked up on foot, burros, and mules.[14]

Queen took advantage of the general's frequent absences to join the growing band of mountaineers, although she mainly limited her outdoor exercise to the ridges and paths of Queen's Canyon. She dressed for those occasions in a free-flowing dress cut amply for hiking, stout boots, and a walking stick tipped with a deer antler. Author Frances Wolcott observed that Mrs. Palmer liked "finding unknown heights and following streams to their sources ... Queen Palmer, climbing stick in hand, rebellious curly hair flying, cheeks aglow, moving as on winged feet, was the spirit incarnate of inaccessible heights. Hats she scorned. She laid claim to beauty as her rightful heritage ..."[15]

Soon Colorado Springs' reputation expanded to include not only tourists but also those seeking a climate to restore their health. Tuberculosis and other respiratory diseases were devastating killers in nineteenth-century Europe and America. Reports of Colorado's arid and generally sunny climate attracted many people in search of relief from their lung diseases. Along with Denver, Colorado Springs became a magnet for desperate consumptive patients.

The most affluent stayed at the Colorado Springs or Manitou Hotel or one of several houses along Tejon and Cascade Avenue. Less prosperous visitors were shuffled off to a row of houses in the north section of town labeled "Dead Man's Row," notable for its invalid residents. Those without means ended up in jail or camped in the hills around Manitou.

Among the more well-heeled visitors was the poet Helen Hunt, who arrived in November 1873 on the advice of her Massachusetts doctor. In addition to bringing a touch of culture to the town, she contributed her unique brand of New England mysticism. Once dubbed by Ralph Waldo Emerson as the "greatest poet in America," Hunt wrote monthly for several magazines including the *Nation* and *Scribner's*. In between her journal articles, she wrote short but important books of poetry. The forty-four-year-old Hunt arrived single but within two years had met and married local businessman Will Jackson, settling into a modest cottage on the corner of Weber and Kiowa Streets. Compared to the skittish and capricious Ms. Hunt, Jackson was a solid, heavily bearded, earthy, upright Quaker and a friend of General Palmer's.

By all accounts the two got on well. The Palmers frequently invited them up to Glen Eyrie, where Queen entertained them with a few songs. Palmer and Jackson talked cards and railroads.

Helen Hunt Jackson was called upon to recite a few of her poems, although evenings were cut short by Helen's "bronchial problems." She wrote some of her best works while convalescing in Colorado Springs. *Bits of Travel at Home* (1878) and *Letters from a Cat* (1879) were well received, but it was not until she left Colorado that her most remarkable works were written, namely *A Century of Dishonor* and *Ramona*. In a savage and polemical work, the former recounted the American government's mistreatment of Native Americans. She traveled widely in California during this time. When *Ramona*, the story of an orphan girl half Indian and half Scots and her struggles in southern California, was published it generated comparisons to Harriet Beecher Stowe's *Uncle Tom's Cabin*, a comparison that Helen particularly embraced.

After Helen's death in 1885 in San Francisco, Will Jackson brought her remains back to Colorado Springs and the scenery she had loved during her stay here. Her legacy as one of the Pikes Peak region's most famous tubercular patients remains to this day.

During the first days of September 1873, Wall Street investors were in a mild panic as shares began slumping. By the morning of September 18, stocks, particularly railroad stocks, began sliding; by the end of the day and into the week they were tobogganing. One of the most important banking systems, Jay Cooke and Company, declared bankruptcy. Cooke's company was heavily invested in railroads and so its collapse meant similar doom for fifty-five other railroad companies. As investors tried to dump shares, the economy went into free fall. To stem the panic, Wall Street was closed for several weeks. The over-extension of railroads after the Civil War had reached its climax, and suddenly the turn of economic events spelled gloom for railroads and their supervising companies. Although the depression hit the East and West Coasts first, it eventually made its way to the Rockies, where Will Palmer sweated out the news at Glen Eyrie.

Other railroads faced similar cutbacks and bankruptcies. At the Union Pacific, where Palmer's nemesis, Jay Gould, had taken over, the economic stalemate meant big projects in and around Colorado were delayed or scrapped entirely. Lingering resentment and suspicion reigned between the two rivals. As a classic robber baron, Gould had used his business acumen to make swindling, bribery, and hostile takeovers part of doing business on Wall Street. He often had his eyes on Colorado and its potential. Standing in the way was William Palmer and his Denver and Rio Grande Railroad, and he was wary of anyone who mentioned Colorado and railroad in the same breath.

The effects of the Panic of '73 were felt in Colorado in 1874 and throughout 1875. Although railroad contracts dried up, there were positive aspects—Palmer's competitors were also precluded from building rails that might threaten his empire. The overall depression impacted the city of Colorado Springs, as growth slowed and so did goods and services. To make matters worse, Queen's father William Mellen died in November 1873. The Palmers, feeling weak and vulnerable, went into mourning. General Palmer maintained that he would take care of the entire Mellen family and he made good on his word. To relieve Palmer of some of the family burden, Mellen's widow, Ellen, insisted that she and her seven children move to a smaller house in Manitou. The Palmers agreed. Will and Queen also felt the pinch of finances. They rented a temporary home for themselves and young Elsie on Cascade Avenue. Glen Eyrie was suddenly abandoned, a victim of the quick cessation of railroad euphoria. Briefly dampened but not defeated were the invincible spirits of Will and Queen Palmer.

Tales of Little London

In the early days of its settlement and founding, Colorado Springs had an infectious case of Anglophilia, a distinction that eventually led to its nickname "Little London." There were several reasons for this nickname. One was the disproportionate amount of British settlers who migrated here—by some estimates forming about 20 percent of the population in the first five years. They brought their customs, traditions, and tea drinking ways with them, and some smuggled into the temperance colony a fifth or two of Dewar's or Old Bushmills. There were also several distinguished British visitors who enjoyed shaping Palmer's little resort town into an English colony out West.

Doctor Willie Bell and Palmer ensured that proper civility and manners would survive in the new city. Doctor Bell had married an English lady, Cora Scovell, and had settled in Colorado Springs while maintaining a home in Britain as well. But possibly the most compelling reason for the traditional use of the name Little London was the proliferation of British architecture and landscape gardens. Although several architectural styles were underway in the western United States—especially after the great Chicago fire of 1871—traditional styles such as early English Gothic and Tudor continued to be favored in Colorado Springs. Americans at the time were obsessed with all things European.

The popularity of Gothic extended well into late nineteenth century on both sides of the Atlantic. The great champion of the form was the English art critic and essayist, John Ruskin, who claimed in two books, *The Seven Lamps of Architecture* and *The Stones of Venice*, that Gothic architecture and its Tudor descendants were the spiritual legacy of the Middle Ages and Renaissance. But Ruskin was not the only advocate. Throughout London and the English countryside were the persistent reminders of the style: Westminster Abbey and Hall and the Houses of Parliament, to name only a few. The reach of Gothic extended into the country's interior with the popularity of country houses, cottages, palaces, and churches. Will Palmer, having absorbed much of the English architecture during his visits, brought his vision for a representative style to his fledgling resort town. Ruskin claimed that Gothic represented the best of Europe's past and exemplified its beliefs in chivalry, honor, duty, sacrifice, and other knightly virtues. The great cavalry hero William Palmer was quick to convert to Gothic and Tudor architecture and made them the prevailing styles for his design of Glen Eyrie. It would be several decades for Will to realize this vision of a country castle, but his dream began in the early days of the city.

In 1874, Palmer donated land to found Colorado College, a school of higher education that in spirit would rival those of the East and Midwest. As the college grew over the years and added buildings, the nucleus of the campus was Gothic, as demonstrated by the erection of Cutler Hall. As time would have it, though, the English Norman (or Romanesque) style found its way into the eclectic mix in Palmer Hall (dedicated 1904). Palmer also founded The Colorado School for the Education of Mutes, which became Colorado Springs School for the Deaf and Blind.

Around town the Gothic design was not just trendy but a sincere belief in the lofty spirit of mankind. Dr. Bell built his home, Briarhurst, in the style, as did early Colorado Springs' residents Irving Howbert and Helen and Will Jackson. Up and down Cascade and North Weber, homes with lancet windows and exposed beams sprouted up in the waning years of the century.

In addition to establishing a predominant style of architecture, Palmer ensured that the gardens of Colorado Springs and Glen Eyrie would be in the finest tradition of landscape design. John Blair hailed from Perthshire, Scotland, and migrated to Colorado Springs after the Chicago fire. He brought with him a tradition of landscape design that included such famous names as Lancelot "Capability" Brown, John Vanbrugh, and William Kent. For Blair, gardens were as essential as the design of the building itself. With his friend Henry Austin, who would later lend his name to Austin Bluffs in the city, the fifty-one-year-old Blair arrived in Palmer's city to begin work beautifying the town. Will Palmer hired him to lay out Manitou Springs and cut a path through Garden of the Gods to facilitate travel. He constructed bridges and "rustic seats placed in appropriate spots."[1]

Blair began an education in Colorado soils, climate, and terrain that would see him through his tenure here and make him the preeminent landscape designer in the city. He encouraged an informal and natural style, one that accentuated the natural beauty of each landscape. Blair was influenced by the work of American horticulturist and Gothic revival advocate A.J. Downing, who in his *Theory and Practice of Landscape Gardening* (1865) distinguished between the beautiful and the picturesque, claiming the latter "aims at the production of outlines of a certain spirited regularity, surfaces comparatively abrupt and broken, and growth of a somewhat wild and bold character." Of course, "wild and bold" gardens were integral to Blair's Colorado landscapes.[2]

Blair discovered that the soil, a dense mixture of clay and sand, could be troublesome. Precipitation was also an issue, varying in one period from eleven inches per year to nearly twenty in the following season. Palmer's gardeners had to haul in manure from Manitou to help improve the soil. Blair also had to work his design around the flash flood-prone area in Queen's Canyon. Two irrigation ditches were dug in 1874 to bring water to the Glen Eyrie gardens. Blair also built rustic stone bridges, ponds, and a carriage house for the Palmers.

Throughout the 1870s, Blair's projects expanded to include the designing of Acadia Park, Alamo Square, Evergreen Cemetery, and the gardens of Dr. Bell's Briarhurst. He also constructed the stone bridge on the road from Colorado City to Denver. While he was supervising these projects, he and his family lived in a cabin overlooking Glen Eyrie, where a host of nearly completed and half-completed projects lay below. Often Will Palmer would ride by on his horse and engage Blair in conversation, or Queen with five-year-old Elsie in tow would stroll by and talk with the gardeners.

Blair spent twenty years in Palmer's employ, designing gardens and landscape features, enduring flash floods, cloudbursts, snowstorms, grasshopper plagues, and withering droughts. Although he left for British Columbia in 1884, where he designed gardens in Victoria and Vancouver, his handiwork will be forever associated with the early years of Glen Eyrie.[3]

While lots in Colorado Springs were selling briskly in the mid- to late-1870s, the Garden of the Gods remained an unspoiled paradise, where tourists and locals alike scrambled over its rock slabs and hiked up its piñon and juniper-covered canyons. Palmer had always admired it, but because it lacked sufficient water, had passed over it in favor of Queen's Canyon. For years writers and artists had marveled at its scenic beauty, and in 1879, Charles Perkins, Palmer's colleague and president of the Chicago, Burlington and Quincy Railroad, purchased it with the idea of building a summer home near the Kissing Camels. Perkins had other homes in the mid-west, and as the Palmer's settled into Glen Eyrie, the four hundred and eighty acre Garden remained pristine and undeveloped—to the relief and delight of all. Two years after Perkins's death in 1907, his children donated the Garden to the city of Colorado Springs.

Charles Kingsley did not have a reputation in America like Dickens, Thackeray, or Tennyson, but when it got out that he would be arriving in Little London in the summer of 1874, word spread quickly. Denver was used to celebrities coming and going; Colorado Springs seemed to puff up like a younger sibling when they arrived. Kingsley had been on a lecture tour of America with daughter Rose. As the canon of Westminster Abbey, one of the most honorable posts in the Church of England, he had a powerful platform from which to speak, but frequently, as a social reformer, his lectures tended to drift into lengthy sermons. Before heading west, he dined with President

Grant in Washington, spoke before The Lotus Club in New York and appreciative audiences in Baltimore, Detroit, Omaha, and St. Louis. In San Francisco he caught a debilitating cold and journeyed to the Springs to recover.

He and Rose arrived at the train depot where they were met by Dr. and Mrs. Bell, the Palmers, and a knot of town officials. Rose had tried to prepare her father for the rigors of a frontier town, but Kingsley was too weary from his cold and his trek across America to be too interested in the place. The Bells nursed and tried to cheer him up in their Briarhurst home. After he was through with his illness, he was invited to Glen Eyrie where the Palmers regaled him with the accomplishments of the town. Kingsley stayed in one the rooms overlooking the glen, too homesick to get enthusiastic about the landscape. "This place is like an ugly Highland strath, bordered with pine woods," he wrote home. "Air almost too fine to breathe. Thank God our time draws nigh. I preach at Colorado Springs tomorrow and lecture for the Church on Wednesday. Denver Friday and right away to New York and embark on July 25 ... I have seen no rattlesnakes, but they killed twenty-five a year or two ago, and little Nat Mellen, twelve years old, killed five ... I will write again before we start over the plain. Oh! Happy day!"[4]

Given the timing of his visit, it was perhaps too much to ask that Kingsley be in great spirits during his sojourn in Palmer's city. The Palmers, however, were buoyed by his brief visit but later saddened by Kingsley's death at age fifty-five the following year. Rose maintained a steady correspondence with Queen, and they remained close throughout the years. It was initially through the Kingsleys that Queen kept a network of friends and acquaintances in England.

During the years 1875–80, while Will was furthering his career in railroads, Queen entered one of the most difficult periods of her life. She withdrew from much of the social life of Colorado Springs to the degree that Marshall Sprague, author of *Newport in the Rockies* (4th edition, 1987), claimed that she was "a beautiful and bittersweet enigma."[5] Sprague contended that Queen never really gave her heart to Colorado Springs and that her true affections were in the social circles of New York and London. But this seems a narrow view of

Queen's needs and ambitions, and one not supported by the evidence just recently made available to writers and historians. Frances Wolcott in her book *Heritage of Years* (1932) suggested that Queen lived "in the third story where she gathered her books, heard musicians, and never permitted any but the invited friend to enter."[6] Queen was in her mid-twenties and seriously re-examining her life. She was married to one of the most important men in Colorado. She had an energetic and inquisitive child to educate. She lived in a modest, seemingly remote castle with a cook and nannies to help with the routines. She had successfully adapted to life in Colorado Springs and the townspeople loved her. But where was Queen Mellen Palmer in all that? She looked at where she had come from and where she was going, listening to the strong mezzo voice that seemed to be always singing inside her, or remembering the many paintings in museums whose colors and outlines lingered in her memory. Part of her loved her life, but another part of her longed for friends, society, art, and music. Must she renounce one to have the other?

In early 1875, the Palmers traveled to Europe and Queen penned one of her last journal entries:

> Four years ago we crossed the ocean. Will and I, when we began a journal as so many people do, thinking that we would keep it up as long as we traveled. We have been traveling nearly constantly since, and the journal so bravely begun came long ago to an untimely and abrupt end!
>
> I began again alone not so boldly, and not with the least faith in my perseverance, a chronicle of the fact and fancies which occur to me as we go. I do this partly to impress more in indelibly on my own mind as I go the marvelous, beautiful, often glorious works I meet every day, very often without looking for them. There is no need, they are there, defying us in their acknowledged grace and beauty.
>
> I have to tell the truth, no plan in this beginning, perhaps I will close this book in disgust when I find how impossible it is for me to describe satisfactorily my impressions. Perhaps instead of chronicling the facts and brief impressions I may find myself, in spite of a fervent desire for the contrary, degenerating into the miserable, well known writer of morbid or even not morbid, egotistical sentimentality with

few facts and many feelings. But after all, what matters it? My pen will only take my first thoughts as they drift through my mind, without weeding. The writing is for myself. Happily I do not need to make an effort in it.[7]

It was not just Queen's life that needed warmth, shape, and color. Elsie was entering her formative years and needed a strong education. The area school was adequate, but Queen wanted more than adequate. Queen realized that Elsie was deeply attracted to her father and life at Glen Eyrie. A bit of a tomboy, Elsie loved the rough and tumble life of a frontier town, sometimes wearing fringed chaps and a cowboy hat, her brunette bangs dangling over her eyes.

As the days passed, Queen felt Elsie's growing attachment to Will and the excitement of her mountain home. Moments of Will's affection for Elsie were plentiful and poignant. After riding in from town, Will would see Elsie walking on the path in her cowboy hat and chaps. Reaching down, he would sweep her onto his horse and the two would lope toward the big house in the glen. Elsie had the large and penetrating eyes of her mother, and Will often stared lovingly into them. Elsie remembered enchanting moments with her father: (274) "We spent hours lying in the soft grasses among the rocks of north Glen Eyrie ... Our mood was a very happy one; we sang, we made up rhymes about the stealing of these hours that should have been spent in town. In the evenings we generally read aloud, and often a talk would begin that lasted very late. At these times he would spread about him a very delightful sense of leisure. Never, not even in the busiest, a slave of time, in moments of relaxation he had—in an extraordinary degree—the gift of enjoying the passing hour and of making others enjoy it."[8]

Queen, too, loved Will dearly, the record is clear, but how she was to reconcile that love with obtaining her needs became the bittersweet dilemma of the rest of her life.

Meanwhile, Will Palmer had his own struggles. As the economic depression eased and business resumed, Palmer and the Denver and Rio Grande began considering additional routes. Their focus turned to southern Colorado as they eyed tracks through the Rockies. Three key areas presented themselves as ripe for commercial development: the first ran west of Pueblo and through the rugged Royal Gorge, which would open the rich lead and silver deposits around Leadville; the second turned west of Walsenburg, headed through La Veta Pass into the Rio Grande Valley; and the third, perhaps the most lucrative, was Raton Pass on the Colorado-New Mexico border, which

The Denver and Rio Grande Railroad Depot, Colorado Springs, in 1890. Courtesy of the Starsmore Center for Local History, Colorado Springs Pioneers Museum.

opened up the entire Southwest, running through Arizona and into the bonanza state of California. While Union Pacific controlled the transcontinental railroad through the northern states, the southern route around the Rockies now became highly desired.

The Atchison, Topeka and Santa Fe (known at the Santa Fe) emerged as Palmer's chief rival. They were also larger, more powerfully organized, and much more able to swat competitors out of the way. The Santa Fe had built its railway across southern Kansas, and rather than turn at Dodge City, had decided to push through the southeast corner of Colorado, following the more lucrative route along the Purgatoire River and cross Raton Pass into New Mexico. The director of operations was William B. Strong, an able and at times ruthless vice president who, like Palmer, fought for supremacy in the often Darwinian world of railroading. In general, the railroad company that made the first and boldest move on a piece of property was granted right of way, and Strong was quick to seize the route through Raton Pass.

The landscape of Colorado south of the Arkansas River differs markedly from the terrain along the Front Range of the Rockies. For one thing it is flat, dry grassland, approaching the hardness of the naked, stony, desert floor. Alkali beds are plentiful and twisting ravines relieve the sameness of the sere landscape all the way from the Arkansas River to Raton Pass. Railroaders loved the terrain because it is flat and workers could lay tracks from sunup to sundown with only a few rattlesnakes and a stray Indian band to worry about.

When Palmer learned that Strong and the Santa Fe were beginning to survey the Raton route, he was incensed. During negotiations with Palmer's railroad, Strong offered not to build through the Royal Gorge if Palmer and the Denver Rio Grande allowed the Santa Fe to lay tracks over Raton and down into Albuquerque. Palmer hesitated. He knew that the Santa Fe wanted both Raton Pass and the Royal Gorge—as he did. Mistrust flourished between the railroad companies. Palmer immediately hired an armed crew to head for Raton Pass and seize

it for the Denver and Rio Grande.

Whether Palmer or Strong and their respective railroads won the right to Raton Pass, the decision ultimately lay with Uncle Dick Wootton, the trader and

A mounted General Palmer circa 1900. Palmer was as an excellent horseman and he is shown here on one of the trails near Glen Eyrie. Courtesy of the Starsmore Center for Local History, Colorado Springs Pioneers Museum.

mountain man who singlehandedly ran a toll road over the pass. A grizzled frontiersman with a mane of tousled gray hair, Wootton had franchises from both Colorado and New Mexico to charge tolls for individuals and groups heading over the pass. Wootton, with help of a band of Ute Indians, had cut a road over the twenty-seven-mile stretch of the pass and had erected a "hotel" at the entrance to waylay travelers, supply them a meal, and administer the fees. He charged $1.50 per wagon and 50 cents for a horseman; Indians were allowed free passage. It was inevitable for Wootton that one day he would have to yield his route to interested railroads, and so he viewed the impending battle between Palmer and Strong as a chance to make a substantial windfall.

Late on a March night in 1878 and acting on orders from the company's management to "seize and hold Raton Pass," two Santa Fe engineers arrived by buckboard at Wootton's hotel. Clad only in a nightshirt and a pair of woolen socks, Wootton opened his door cradling a shotgun.[9] The agents negotiated a financial settlement with Wootton for use of his pass by the Santa Fe Railroad, a settlement that would give Wootton a monthly income and a free pass on the Santa Fe line.

They also pressed Wootton to hire a gang of workers to start grading the pass, hoping to establish a claim over the route by right of execution. Wootton agreed to help them recruit as many men as they needed, even rounding up workers in nearby Trinidad to swell their numbers. Within days, a gang of several hundred men bearing picks, shovels, and lanterns trudged up the pass. Some carried pistols and rifles, as reports that Palmer and the Denver and Rio Grande were also in the vicinity endeavoring to make their claim.

In truth, a rough group of several hundred Denver and Rio Grande construction men, many well armed, were only a short distance behind the Santa Fe workers. Palmer monitored operations from his office in Pueblo, firing out telegrams and hiring riders to carry cryptic messages down to his crew approaching Raton Pass. Palmer was at his best in such situations. Driven by anger and pumped with adrenalin, he mustered all his diplomatic and survival skills to keep the routes in Colorado for himself and his company.

When the fight for Raton Pass seemed imminent, he headed by train and horseback for the New Mexico border to personally oversee the battle between railroad companies. As he anticipated action, Palmer tried to look as formidable as possible, stiffening his wiry frame, wearing his cowboy hat at a rakish angle, and donning his polished riding boots to appear taller. Not since the Civil War had the fighting spirit been so strong in Will. He had sensed it briefly during the survey of the Southwest in the 1860s when he fended off the Apaches in Arizona, but presently it overtook him as he led his raffish band of men up the pass to encounter his rivals.

The Santa Fe party saw Palmer and his men approaching. When the former reached the spot where they were to begin grading, they erected a hastily built barricade of sticks and fallen timber to block Palmer's way. Palmer had his hand on his holstered pistol, while two of his henchmen had their weapons fully drawn. Palmer's men reached the barricade and stopped. Over the breastwork, perhaps forty yards away, stood a grim line of Santa Fe workers and conscripts.

The March morning had broken clear and cold. A standoff ensued, during which both groups hurled insults and threats at each other. Will quickly realized the situation: the Santa Fe had armed possession of the pass and had established priority by execution. He could fight but both sides would take substantial casualties. Most courts in the land would support the Santa Fe's right to build through Raton Pass. He also knew that Strong and the Santa Fe, after having taken the pass, would next target the Royal Gorge. Saving his men and his resources for that battle seemed a more discreet choice.

Wisely, Will Palmer had his men holster their weapons, shoulder their picks and shovels, and head back down the pass, where they would board the train for Pueblo and prepare for the fight at the Royal Gorge.

Queen and six-year-old Elsie felt the tension of the railroad wars within the walls of Glen Eyrie. Queen knew when to stay out of Will's way, especially if she heard some blistering conversation coming from his study. More often than not, however, Will was the occasional husband, spending his time in Pueblo, Denver, or back East drumming up support for the D&RG.

He had little time now for horseback rides in the Garden of the Gods or in Queen's Canyon. He mounted all his efforts to secure the Royal Gorge, which he knew would be critical for his railroad's future success.

At least for the first decade of their marriage, Queen took Will's business absences in stride. She went about her business ensuring the town's schools were adequately supplied with good teachers. She met dignitaries as they arrived in town, such as the whirlwind stop in 1875 by President Ulysses Grant, Will's former commander in chief. Glen Eyrie remained a safe haven with its oaks, cottonwoods, and its towering rock skyscrapers. The grounds were a perfect, cloistered place to walk, and in the morning to see the wildlife, including deer and mountain goats, stalk down to feed on the buffalo grass and at night to see a heaven of stars sprinkled across the sky. But there were concerns. Will openly feared that hostilities with the Santa Fe Railroad might lead to threats against his family. He told Queen to be extra vigilant of Elsie, worried that the Santa Fe might try to kidnap her for ransom or threaten her life. Will also expressed concern that the Mellen family, who still lived in Manitou, might be similarly threatened.

Queen maintained a brisk correspondence with Fanny and Rose Kingsley. Through the Kingsleys she was introduced to a wide strata of British society, including writers, painters, socialites, and politicians. One of those personalities was Alma Strettel, a twenty-eight-year-old poet, translator, and friend to writers Henry James, Edmund Gosse, George Meredith, and the painter John Singer Sargent. Both Strettel and Queen loved operas, particularly those of Richard Wagner. Strettel became instrumental to Queen's introduction to British high society, but she also was important in obtaining for her brother an invitation to travel to Colorado Springs to recuperate from a severe respiratory infection. Queen offered Alma and her brother a room at Glen Eyrie while he convalesced. Queen was pleased that she could reciprocate Alma's generosity and goodwill.

As the decade wore on, Queen became increasingly attracted to English society, its eccentricities, its high drama and drab vulgarity, its strong and fake allegiances. Her correspondence with her European friends kept her in touch with the vibrant world of late Victorian England and gave her life in Colorado its meaning and purpose. By contrast, life at Glen Eyrie had low cultural voltage and limited social traffic, but it was her home and she determined to make the best of it.

Meanwhile, General Palmer had a fight on his hands. Although it was alluring, the Royal Gorge was a nightmare to survey and construct a railroad through. From its rim, the gorge plunged 1,250 feet straight down; its base was fifty feet across and about a hundred feet at its top; it was roughly ten miles long with only a shelf on the floor wide enough for one set of tracks. Chunky pink granite made it difficult to blast through or pick with an axe. It was beautiful, rugged, and dangerous.

In mid-April 1878, less than a month after the dispute at Raton Pass, both armed railroad gangs moved to the top of the Royal Gorge hoping to secure a toehold on the canyon floor. The Santa Fe had begun grading at the mouth of the canyon, but Palmer and his men stopped them from proceeding farther. Brief volleys of rifle fire echoed through the sharp dry air as the two gangs kept each other at bay. All equipment and supplies had to be lowered from the rim down to the floor of the canyon, so that process continued while the gangs took shots at each other.

The conflict known as the Royal Gorge War lasted two years. Most of it was punctuated by shouts, gunfire, and threats at the canyon while the lawyers for the two companies sought legal action to clear the way for their respective corporations. Both companies wanted the bonanza at Leadville—its silver and lead deposits and the possibility that one day it would be the center of commerce for the Rockies. Will directed operations from the canyon rim, but frequently left for his office in Pueblo or a heavily guarded locomotive in Cañon City.

The standoff at the gorge and the legal wrangling took a heavy emotional toll on Palmer. He was somewhat relieved when in April 1879, the Denver and Rio Grande won the legal right to build through the gorge. The Santa Fe countered that it would continue building through the gorge. Because of declining earnings and the fear of the stockholders, Palmer's railroad offered to lease its rails in the gorge to the Santa Fe for thirty years. The decision of the D&RG stockholders to give in to the Santa Fe Railroad went against the best personal interests of Will Palmer, but he reluctantly signed the lease giving the Santa Fe access to the interior wealth of the Rockies.

During the summer of 1879, earnings at D&RG slipped significantly, so the company went to court to break their lease with the Santa Fe. The Denver and Rio Grande sought to take back their right of way to the Royal Gorge and begin generating income again. Armed gangs of Palmer's men muscled their way into the Santa Fe offices in Cañon City and Pueblo. More gunfights ensued at the gorge. The Santa Fe hired anybody who could carry a gun at the rate of five to ten dollars a day to join their army of twelve hundred men. Cowboys, miners, drifters, and drunks thrown out of the saloons in Pueblo showed up at the canyon site. Two men more fashionably dressed than the others also arrived, Bat Masterson and Doc Holliday. Wearing bowler hats and with Colt revolvers stuck in their waistbands, the pair traveled from Dodge City to add ammunition to the Santa Fe's cause. Other hired guns included "Mysterious" Dave Mather, Ben Thompson, and "Dirty" Dave Rudabaugh. They tried to coerce a friend, Eddie Foy, to join them, but he declined because he couldn't shoot straight in a fight.

While much testosterone and many bullets were expended during the war—although no one was killed—ultimately the courts in Denver and Washington decided the case, ruling that the Denver and Rio Grande had the legal right to Royal Gorge. The D&RG paid the Santa Fe $1.8 million for the equipment and partial rail lines it had already completed and began laying its own track to Leadville. The first Palmer locomotive and train chugged into the mining town in July 1880. Although Palmer had lost a few battles in the struggle, he had ultimately won the war.

At over 10,000 feet above sea level, Leadville, Colorado, was a brawny town tabbed by General Palmer as the crown jewel in his quest to capitalize on the abundant resources of the Rockies. Like many mountain towns, it had rough beginnings. Carlyle Channing, who began editing the upstart newspaper the *Chronicle*, noted that the "main thoroughfare was pretty closely and compactly lined with houses on either side, for a distance of two miles following the contour of the gulch, all of log or roughhewn slab construction. Every other door was a saloon, dance hall, or gambling den. There were no street lights, but thousands of coal oil lamps indoors cast fitful flashes of baneful light across the way."[10]

Down the street and around the corner from the tattoo shop and the Red Light Hall saloon was the building for the Leadville Literary Society, which stocked copies of Charles Dickens, Jules Verne, Alexander Dumas, and Wilkie Collins. As summers were brief at this elevation, the society was often quite a busy place through the colder months of September through May.

Backed by mine owners Horace Tabor and August Meyer, the hamlet surged in population, so that by 1880 it boasted 14,000 souls, second only to Denver. Amid the ramshackle cabins and instant store fronts, Horace Tabor built his opera house in 1879, an elegant, colorful structure dripping in Victorian lace and fringes that helped boost Leadville's growing reputation as a major theater and arts town. It managed to attract a sprinkling of celebrities and entertainers during the 1880s, including the quixotic Anglo-Irish dandy, Oscar Wilde.

Normally a place such as Leadville would not attract sophisticated ladies, but in the summer of 1880, Queen and her visiting English friend, Alma Strettel, set out from Glen Eyrie in one of Palmer's trains for a sightseeing trip to the silver mining town. It was not the safest journey for a pair of women alone, but Queen put her fear aside, packed one of Will's revolvers in a picnic basket, and left with Miss Strettel on the roughly 130-mile trip into the heart of the Rockies.

Alma Strettel became one of Queen's dearest companions, largely through her gracious and lively sojourn in Colorado. Her brother stayed in the healing atmosphere at Glen Eyrie, and later in Colorado Springs. Alma and Queen were fascinated by stories of Tabor's opera house and longed to see it in person. The rage for opera was at its height in both America and Europe at this time, to the degree that over 150 opera houses were built in Colorado by the turn of the twentieth century.

On the return trip, Queen felt a stabbing pain her heart, the first of several attacks in her life that were the result of an inherited condition. Queen and the doctors she consulted blamed Colorado's high elevation and consequently the lack of oxygen for her circulatory system. The moment of her heart attack brought the thirty-year-old Mrs. Palmer face to face with a grim reality: she would have to leave her beloved Glen Eyrie home or the face the prospect of death. She thought of Elsie and Will. She confronted the painful truth that Will might not understand and continue with his life without her. She did not want to die at some innocent moment by insisting on living in the Colorado Rockies, and so she endured the most difficult and stressful condition that any human had to undergo: the heart in conflict with itself.

English Hours

For the next five years following her heart attack, Queen Palmer engaged in an anxious pilgrimage in search of a healthy climate. During this time she did not abandon Glen Eyrie entirely, but she did restrict her activity around the property. She accompanied Will on several trips to New York and England, where she became reacquainted with her circle of British friends. In October 1880, she gave birth to Dorothy Palmer and over a year later, while in England, to Marjory in November 1881. Throughout her physical difficulties in the early 1880s and beyond, Will reassured her that he would always financially and emotionally support her and the children no matter where they lived. When the family traveled, they were usually accompanied by two maids, a cook, two governesses, and the family doctor.

Her sojourns at Glen Eyrie became increasingly difficult. Her doctor had ruled out horseback riding and strenuous hiking. She had trouble sleeping and often she stayed in her room on the third floor, reading, sewing, and surveying the sweep of the glen from her window. The children were often dissuaded from seeing her when she was not feeling well.

The sometimes severe Colorado winters were now out of the question, as she found periodic solace in some of the cities on the East Coast. Her greatest fear was that death would catch her unawares, preventing her from seeing to the welfare of her children.

In addition to Will and Queen, the other victim of Queen's

health dilemma was ten-year-old Elsie. She loved horses and rode constantly when in Colorado or England. Her love of animals and nature matched that of Will's. She began, however, to feel the disruption of the Palmer marriage, being shuffled here and shepherded there. She had a loving and compliant spirit, which enabled her to adapt to most difficult situations. She began to resist the world of her mother as it impinged on the realm of her father. It became natural and instinctual for her to choose sides in certain situations, and as she entered her teens

From the left Dorothy, Marjory, and Elsie Palmer in 1883. Courtesy of the Starsmore Center for Local History, Colorado Springs Pioneers Museum.

this split in allegiances became even more pronounced. At one level she understood her mother's health issues, but on another, deeper level her heart did not want to consider such rational explanations. It craved safety, harmony, and reassurance.

Will traveled frequently by himself. His company, now reorganized under the name of the Rio Grande Western, had extended its lines to Salt Lake City and Ogden. He was periodically in Mexico, trying once again to establish a route from America to Mexico City. He wrote Queen from New York in 1882, cautioning her not to encourage Elsie to grow up too quickly: "There is a hot house tendency nowadays on our ideas about children, as if the competitions of the business and social world had entered the nursery and the schoolhouse, and too little of the slow healthy growth which permits the best developments through all the stages of the body and mind. We are so ambitious for her that we may have driven her too much, in our anxious zeal, and made a little machine of her."[1]

In another letter, written aboard ship, he addressed her as "My Darling Queenie ... I have taken it easy aboard ship ... I shall plunge into the maelstrom however tomorrow. My single purpose now is to rescue the various enterprises from the gulf which seems to yawn for them and save my friends and the other investors from a final loss if possible ... My little family is the oasis—the only green spot to which my mind can turn without distress and disappointment ... And you my dear wife whom I have so often cruelly distressed and whose affections I allowed to be estranged because I was hard and cold and blind and stupid and wretchedly wrong altogether, and reckless at a heaven would life seem now, if with vigorous health, one had nothing to do but start without a penny to make a home for this beloved flock."[2]

At another time he wrote Elsie directly wishing her a happy Christmas but lamenting he was "all alone again."[3]

Between 1884 and 1886, Queen made only brief appearances in Colorado, the last being in late 1886. After leaving Newport, Rhode Island, she settled into an apartment in the newly built Dakota Hotel overlooking Central Park in New York City. With its towering gables and imposing façade, the Dakota quickly became a central landmark in the Manhattan skyline. Adding to the fervor of life in New York was the completion of the Brooklyn Bridge and the arrival in 1885 of sections of the Statue of Liberty.

The Dakota Hotel—so named because it was erected in the then remote hinterland of the Upper West Side—possessed many modern features such as elevators, electricity, and central heating, which attracted the more affluent guests. Meals were sent up to residents by dumbwaiters. When Queen and her children settled in, the Dakota had sixty-five apartments with most rooms furnished in the latest décor. Each room and apartment was different from the other and paneled in mahogany, oak, and cherry. In winter, Queen's three daughters peered out at the children and adults ice skating in the park below.

When Will happened to be in town he went back and forth between his office at 11 Broadway and the Dakota. He brought news of the new hotel gracing the horizon of downtown Colorado Springs, the

Marjory Palmer in the late 1880s. Courtesy of the Starsmore Center for Local History, Colorado Springs Pioneers Museum.

Queen with Dorothy in 1886, just before Queen and her daughters left for England. Courtesy of the Starsmore Center for Local History, Colorado Springs Pioneers Museum.

Antlers, which was managed by Dr. Bell. Like the Dakota, the Antlers featured modern conveniences for the weary traveler. The turreted, Queen Anne–style Antlers offered elevators, public rooms, and Turkish baths. General Palmer was particularly proud of it because it gave him a tangible and elegant edifice to support the hyperbole of his advertising.[4]

While New York winters were not as cold as Colorado's, four feet of snow piled up on the steps of the Dakota during the winter of 1885–86. The frigid temperatures and wind howling off the East River chilled her to the bone. Elsie and Dorothy came down with colds. Although the ensuing spring enabled the family to go out on the croquet lawns, Queen was barely able to endure the harsh winters.

Elsie missed her Colorado home, expressing her longing in stories and reminisces. In one story titled "A Magic Wand," two siblings wish for a sorcerer's wand and soon find themselves underwater amid strange creatures that change shape and size before their eyes. In a second story "Man Overboard," she describes an incident on the voyage from England to America, during which her family plus two governesses watched a man slip over the rail and drift into the ocean. Elsie details how the ship turned around and brought the man to safety. She describes Coney Island and New York City, but emphasizes her homesickness for Colorado. When she finally boarded the train for Colorado Springs, she wrote that, "I was so glad I did not know what to do. It seemed to me that I was never going to get home ... I thought that I never wanted to go away from Glen Eyrie again."[5] She drifted into childhood memories, recalling the scent of her father's boots: "These boots lived in a cupboard in his bedroom, and into this cupboard I had once been put because I was naughty. It was not a severe punishment, for I remember the experience as odd and interesting—sitting in the dark which was filled with the rather pleasant leathery smell of the boots."[6]

While her younger sisters' memories of Glen Eyrie were shadowy, Elsie's remained vivid during her adolescence. She remembered the afternoon walks with her father in Queen's Canyon: "We spent hours lying in the soft grasses among the rocks of north Glen Eyrie, where the flowers were growing thick—harebells, red pentstemon, kinnikinnick, and painter's brush. Our mood was a very happy one; we sang, we made up rhymes about the stealing of the hours that should have been spent in town ..."[7]

Elsie also sent a letter to children's author George Macdonald describing how much his books meant to her and of her home out West in America. "Our home in Colorado is in the midst of the mountains and a long way off from houses, and I love it

Queen with Elsie, 1886. Courtesy of the Starsmore Center for Local History, Colorado Springs Pioneers Museum.

more than any other place in the world. Some of your descriptions in your books remind me very much of it; and when I go far away to the beautiful red rocks, they help me understand them."[8] Clearly her father, Colorado, and Glen Eyrie had a substantial effect on Elsie. She kept a blank book in which she kept letters from her favorite authors and notes revealing her fondness for the foothills and canyons of the Rockies.

After two severe winter seasons in New York, Queen decided that southern England would be the place she would settle. Encouraging her in this move were the Kingsleys, Alma Strettel, Alma's sister Alice, and Alice's husband, the influential art critic Joseph Comyns Carr. With public funds and her strong belief in education, Rose Kingsley had started the Leamington High School for young women and was anxious for Queen to see her project. Several of the Mellen family had drifted toward England for their education, so Queen had additional support for the move. In early 1887, she took her last view of New York harbor, the newly erected Statue of Liberty, and with her three daughters sailed for a new life in England.

Ightham Mote, near Seven Oaks, Kent. The Mote was the Palmer's residence from 1887-1890. (Public domain)

After scouting several properties in Sussex and Kent, Queen settled on a five-hundred-year-old medieval, stone and half-timbered house near Tonbridge Wells, called Ightham Mote (pronounced "item moot"). The house seemed straight out of the Middle Ages and Camelot, and it retained its magic for Elsie and Queen during their entire stay there. It had a walled courtyard where residents and guests could stroll safely. A moat swirled around its massive walls, giving it an air of serene timelessness. While her mother negotiated the lease agreement inside, Elsie walked the grounds and sat under a fir tree with a view of the moat and turreted outbuildings. "This is a very nice old place," fourteen-year-old Elsie noted in her diary.[9]

Queen found a Europe alive with new ideas and lively personalities. One of its main currents was the aesthetic movement in the arts, a movement that filtered into many aspects of British life, including painting, the decorative arts, theater, and education. Essentially the aesthetic movement was a belief in the cult of beauty and that great art need not have any social, political, or moral implications. It was a rejection of the values of one of the century's great art critics, John Ruskin, who in books such as *Modern Painters* (1843) and *Seven Lamps of Architecture* had argued that art, in order for it be meritorious, must have some grounding in moral values.

For four decades Ruskin's views dominated English and European art, but by the end of the 1870s a new generation of painters and poets were quick to declare that art and morality were independent of each other, and that a painting or a poem must be judged solely on it intrinsic merits. Artists flaunted the idea that beauty was at last free of any moral or social baggage.

The main practitioners of this cult of aestheticism included Oscar Wilde, the poet Algernon Charles Swinburne, art critic Walter Pater, and artist James Whistler. In the theater, Gilbert and Sullivan sometimes promoted and often satirized the movement's excesses in such operettas as *Patience* (1881). Queen loved the music from these light operas and was often singing their whimsical tunes in the garden of her house. Two of the movement's fringe supporters and ones that would figure significantly in the lives of Queen and her daughters were the great American novelist Henry James and the Anglo-American painter John Singer Sargent. Both James and Sargent shared Queen's and Will's love of all things English, including afternoon tea, scones, and a touch of village gossip.

Henry James was in his mid-forties and already a celebrated novelist when he first met the Palmers. As one of America's best gifts to English letters, he early demonstrated great literary skill in *The Portrait of a Lady* (1881). His works examined the clash of cultures, the often glaring and sometimes subtle differences between American and British society. His heroines were frequently young women with uncertain destinies who were brought to England by well-meaning but often incompetent parents. The corpulent and balding novelist circulated in both London society and among the vast network of country houses in southern England, where he carefully listened to people's conversations and intently watched their expressions, gaining in the process some insight into their true selves versus how they appeared on the surface. He was probably our most ardent eavesdropper, turning his findings into sharp and sparkling dialogue in his novels.

Among his sphere of friends was the painter John Singer Sargent, who after years in Paris arrived in London in 1886 at the request of James to set up his studio on Tite Street. James had implored him to try London society: "Come here to live and work—there being such a field in London for a real painter of women."[10] Only his early thirties, Sargent had proven himself to be one of the great portrait painters of his age. By the time he came to London, he had already left a record worthy of a superb painter. His triumphs included such works as *El Jaleo* (1882), *Lady with a Rose* (1882), *The Daughters of Edward D. Boit* (1882), and the sensational *Madam X* (1884), which caused a scandal at the Paris Salon for the daring treatment of its subject. Henry James praised Sargent for "the quality in the light of which the artist sees deep into his subject, undergoes it, absorbs it, and discovers new things that were not on the surface ... elevates it and humanizes the technical problem."[11] Aspiring socialites, celebrities, artists, writers, and debutantes sought to be painted by the current master of the portrait.

The London cultural scene was a close-knit fraternity of artists, writers, critics, and theater people, and perhaps no couple was more central to Queen Palmer's introduction to London society than the Carrs, who became regular guests at Ightham Mote. Alice Strettel Carr was a noted fashion designer who created the dress worn by actress Ellen Terry for her famous role as Lady Macbeth. As Alma's sister, she became a confidante to Queen and later to Elsie, Dorothy, and Marjory Palmer. Sargent painted portraits of both Alma and Alice, the latter in her Lady Macbeth costume. J. Comyns Carr held several important positions including critic, art gallery director, playwright, and theater manager. His New Gallery in London promoted the work of the Pre-Raphaelites—Rossetti, Burne-Jones, and Whistler—who sought a return to the aesthetic values before the Renaissance. As a theater manager he wrote and directed several important plays in the medieval vein, including the popular *King Arthur*. Sargent and James circulated in the Carr's orbit, and by the summer of 1887 both had been introduced by Alma Strettel and the Carrs to Queen Palmer.

Residents and guests found the seventy-room Ightham Mote a strange old relic that produced a number of reactions. To Elsie and her sisters it was a medieval fantasy where jousting knights clashed out in the paddock and ladies in flowing dresses roamed the darkened hallways. The Mote came with a serious ghost story. According to the legend, one of the original owners, Dame Dorothy Selby, was a diehard Catholic who learned of the Gunpowder Plot to blow up Parliament in 1605. She sent a letter to her cousin, Lord Monteagle, warning him to stay away from the place. After the letter was intercepted, Dorothy became implicated in the plot, and the King's supporters had her walled up in one of the rooms behind the chimney. Her ghost was said to wander the hallways and provide the chilly drafts that appeared even in summer. In 1872, workers discovered her skeleton tied to a chair behind one of the wood panels. Within months, the ghost tale of Ightam Mote spread across the county of Kent. With several embellishments over the years, the story remained an eerie tale for the Palmer sisters to mull over on a winter evening,[12]

Henry James was a master of the psychological ghost story, a genre that developed in England and America from the Gothic novel of the eighteenth and nineteenth centuries. James stayed at the Mote several times and promoted its haunted image. On a two-night stay in 1887, he related that he "slept in a room with a ghost and an oubliette, but fortunately the former remained in the latter." He found the grounds "in a state of almost perilous decrepitude."[13] His views underscored the plight of many ancient country houses under the ownership of cash-strapped British heirs who turned to wealthy Americans to finance their homes' restoration. But since the Palmer's were only renting, the house awaited a new set of owners to begin modifications and improvements.

James remained a lifelong friend of Queen and later her three daughters until his death in 1917. He kept up a correspondence with Mrs. Palmer and periodically checked on her welfare.[14]

Although the winters turned damp and rain settled in for days, Queen found her new home highly suitable for her health issues and the children's upbringing. She frequently wrote Will summarizing their days at the Mote. In one letter she noted that, "this place is full of the most delicious fruit—so we wish very much that you were here to help us eat it. The peaches are delicious—this is a great thing for the children."[15] In another letter Queen reported that, "the children are in excellent health. Dorothy especially is fat and her skin looks brighter and smoother and healthier than it ever has looked." She continued on to say that periodic visits to Eastbourne and other coastal towns helped improve their health and their outlook. "Elsie has never been so interested in her work—and as for the babies they dance with delight at the mere thought of going to school."[16] Although Queen did not directly monitor the daily lessons delivered by the governesses, she always stressed the traditional virtues

Henry James. Charcoal sketch by John Singer Sargent, 1912. James was a dear friend of Mrs. Palmer while she was in England. (Public domain)

of loyalty, empathy, sincerity, duty, and a love for beautiful things.

She discovered that southern England, especially living at the Mote, fulfilled some of her deepest yearnings for safety, security, and connection to the outside world, leading to the belief among some historians that the English sojourn signaled a fracture in the Palmer's marriage. But this was not the case. The evidence of Queen's and Will's correspondence reveals a healthy separation in their marriage that allowed both of them the space to become themselves and fulfill their own needs. In a letter of July 9, 1887, Queen wrote: "Now about my health as regards future plans. I had a thorough examination made by Dr. Sedgwick and told him about my house in Colorado—and my desire to get back to it as soon as possible. He said that in his opinion I should not attempt it for another two years." In the same letter she mentioned that Switzerland might be another option "but only for a short time. So I have the opportunity of going and being taken care of with Miss Strettel and the Jamiesons if I decide to go."

In another missive, perhaps unsent, Queen lays out for Will her deepest desire to be healthy and at the same time return to Colorado to be with him:

> And now my dear Will about my health and the prospect of being able to live in America.
>
> I gave you the opinion of the three physicians who know my trouble best when I wrote to you a few months ago—and nothing has happened since to change their opinion. That New York is on a level with the sea is quite true—but the strain of the climate even there might be fatal for me at present. The very thing in this English climate, which is called relaxing for some people—is the quality most favorable for my condition which as I think I wrote you—is more sensitive for the next few years [seven or eight crossed out], than it will be afterward. If the children were older—I should not hesitate to try—notwithstanding their opinions for I might do well enough and if I did not—it wouldn't make much difference but as it is—I want to see them grown up— if possible ... But I will not let you be so homeless any more—if you cannot come to us—Elsie must make a home for you there. You know how decidedly fond of you she is.

Is it impossible for you to come to England?—with only an occasional visit to America?

Can you not give up some of your responsibilities there—and with a smaller income in consequence—be happy with your little family here—I should look for a house a little larger than this—in a beautiful part of the country—where we all could be so happy together—and then—after a few years that I ought to remain here—we might all be able to go back to our home in Glen Eyrie, for the doctors say that after these years, if I get well enough with them I will be better than I have been since that attack of bronchitis in New York ... Do consider this well—it would be a rest for you, too, that would probably do you good, as well. If you say so—I could look about and find our little house and be all ready for you when you come next.[7]

Whether Will received such a letter is not known. If he did, he did not act on her suggestions, possibly because he believed that a move from Glen Eyrie was out of the question. He did, however, maintain an enduring love and respect for her needs.

While at the Mote, Queen could be extravagant in her costumes and "dress-ups" without being an exhibitionist. Living twenty-five miles from the heart of London and having such acquaintances as Alma Strettel, Mrs. Comyns Carr, and actress Ellen Terry allowed Queen important connections to both the theatrical and fashion worlds. Ellen Terry was the most celebrated Shakespearean actress in the theater world during this time. In addition to playing Lady Macbeth, she was known for roles as Portia in *The Merchant of Venice* and Ophelia in *Hamlet*. Her off-stage antics and dramatic episodes with reporters were legend. With Alice Comyns Carr she shared a love for fashion directly tied to the London stage. Hence, Ightham Mote was frequently a place to demonstrate the latest costumes bound for the boards of the West End.

The ladies were also fond of acting out certain scenes from both modern and Elizabethan drama. Queen was often called upon to sing arias from Wagner by donning a flamboyant costume that included a "feathered helmet, large shield, and body armor." Alice Comyns Carr remembered Queen for her love of the picturesque, "especially in the matter of clothes, and one of our favorite pastimes was to design clothes which would harmonize with the character of the house."[18] Thus, all things medieval—art, dress, theater—were celebrated and encouraged at the Mote.

Given the degree of Queen's love of medieval and renaissance lore, there was no question that Glen Eyrie would be finished and outfitted in English Gothic.

William Palmer visited England two times a year, usually once in summer and again during the Christmas holidays. Word of his coming excited both the family and the staff at the Mote. "While he was there," wrote John Fisher in his 1939 biography of Palmer, "there was a bustle of coming and going—a breath of electric Colorado air in the calm English days; there were the business talks, the rides, the meals delayed, the catholic crowding of guests; the games of "circus" with the little girls ..."[19]

The period 1883–1887 were years of uncertainty and triumph for Will Palmer in Colorado. He had been forced out of the presidency of the Denver and Rio Grande Railroad in August 1883 by a board of directors who blamed him for over-extending the routes and squandering the capital of the investors. He held on long enough to extend the rails into Utah, but soon thereafter the company went into receivership. Construction was halted on all the routes and jobs were cut. While this slowdown occurred, Palmer revived hopes of establishing a Mexican national railroad. His friend, Mexican President Diaz, had opened the door for such a venture by making rail travel safer and more attractive to American investors. With the Mexican government's encouragement and Palmer's financial support and planning, the Mexican Central Railway (later the National Railroad of Mexico) was created. Although Palmer never realized the dream of laying his own tracks into Mexico, his assistance was critical in establishing a federal rail system in the country.

Will had much to boast about when he visited Queen and the girls in December 1887. The Mote was decorated festively and his daughters had new dresses. Ellen Terry, Mrs. Comyns Carr, John Sargent, and Alma Strettel stopped in at various times during the season to drink a glass of mulled cider with Queen and Will. Henry James was also invited and he described the Christmas sojourn as "a queerly uncomfortable yet entertaining visit with General Palmer, a Mexican railway man and his wife and children ... the episode was the drollest amalgam of American and Western characteristics in the rarest old English setting."[20] At this time, the couple did present a rather interesting contrast for their English guests: Will, now in his early fifties, garbed in riding boots and cowboy hat, his ginger-colored mustache brushed wistfully back from his lip; Queen dressed in a Regent Street original or something colorful borrowed from Ellen Terry's wardrobe. It should be noted, however, that James at other times was quite fond of the couple and found their successful life in American railroads inspiring.

By her thirty-eighth birthday in March 1888, Queen showed more worrisome sings of fatigue and dizziness. She rarely complained, however, saving her most intimate concerns for her diary and for a friend such as Alma Strettel over a cup of tea. She often felt compelled to share her fears with her daughters in a letter meant to be read after her death:

> My precious three little girls—mother wants to be very sure you have some words from her—for "God Speed"—in case she should be called away suddenly on a long journey without time to speak them to you before she goes ... you will listen to them I know and will remember them for her sake ... Be true ... be kind ... be gentle and brave—to a hand outstretched to any soul who may be helped by it—as you freely give be generous to receive. With an everlasting kiss from your precious lips— my three own babies, my own, own ones—I say to you—for Motherling is with you—forever—only you don't see her—you will remember how she loves you ... God be with you.[21]

But Queen's overall health improved slightly while in England, and by the following spring she felt energetic enough to accompany Will on a trip to the Continent. Will had planned it as a celebration of their courtship, engagement, and twenty-year marriage. This time, however, he would forego business meetings and concentrate solely on enjoying his time with Queen. Will sailed from America and met Queen at the Mote, beginning their trip on March 8, 1889. Leaving the children with their governesses, the couple left the train station at Tonbridge Wells and headed to catch the packet boat at Dover.

In addition to feeling better physically, Queen enjoyed a restoration of their relationship, which had been made more difficult by the months of separation. Her 1889 journal also shows a remarkable and spirited approach to life—one that would sustain her regardless of the time she had left. Her incisive verbal sketches and brief snapshots of European life indicate she intended to make the trip a success for both of them.

After landing in France, they headed to Paris in a carriage "with five other ladies—all whom became intimate within an hour! I bury myself in the *New American* with an occasional interruption when something is too good not to share with [Will] who always understands."[22]

In Paris she found that the Rue Lafayette reminded her of Broadway and once at their hotel she discovered that General Palmer had booked a room on the lower level "to save [her] the stairs."

Their stops in Paris included the Maison de Louvre, much to Queen's delight for she could leave the many shops and flee "into the open arms of Art." Invited to dinner at a friend's apartment, she was lifted up the stairs in a chair especially designed for her visit. "It is hoped that the shrinking from physical dependence will soon be gone," she noted.[23]

On March 10 they boarded a train for southern France, pausing in Avignon to walk through the cathedral and see frescoes by Simone Memmi. Shortly thereafter in Marseilles, a "dreary place," according to Queen, they visited the museum and stood before "a pretty Perugino and a doubtful Corot." Since Corot was one of the most forged artists of the nineteenth century, many fake Corots turned up in European museums.

They wrote their daughters from the hotel, and afterward headed to the Italian coast and Doria Castle, near La Spezia, where Queen was especially attracted to the light. "I wish I could give an idea of the wonderful effect of the light and color—with sparkling brilliancy of the atmosphere, and the delicious feeling of light and air ... It had some of the quality of Colorado air, just as the scenery was dimly suggestive of Colorado."[24]

They passed through many coastal towns with their ancient cobblestone byways, little ochre chapels, sun-washed plazas, all perched above a cerulean and milk sea. Queen and Will reveled in the strength of the health-giving sun and the brilliance of the colors.

Before reaching Monte Carlo, the two discussed the benefits and of gambling, to which Queen had an initial attraction. They entered one casino, deciding "they would do nothing but look at the players." Gold and bank notes lay in little heaps on the table as the players nervously eyed their next move. "And the horrid game goes on," noted Queen, "for it is repulsive to me ... how could I have possibly found a remote desire to put down anything on the tables?" They moved to a darker room where the "light of day is closed out by closely drawn curtains and they are playing by *lamplight!*" They raced for the doors of the casino. "It has become too painful for us—it reminds one strangely of a tropical growth of parasites."[25]

Later in Genoa they attended a performance of *Hamlet* or "Amleto," which they found full of "useless vehement emotion." They left in the middle of the play and "drew a sigh of relief when we were safely in their carriage."[26]

For Queen's thirty-ninth birthday they were in Florence, one of the great cities of the Renaissance, where Will took communicating rooms in a little pensione, so "they could each indulge our little eccentricities without disturbing the other." Overwhelmed with the art and architecture in a city that hosted Michelangelo, Botticelli, Donatello, and Raphael, she felt instantly refreshed. Her heart never felt healthier, her stamina never stronger, her soul never more aroused. On March 29, she penned in her journal: "I must begin my day's journal by saying that I *am almost wild with delight. A new hunger is discovered in me*—by myself which has been gradually growing—ever since I left Nice—and it has reached its climax in this great—beautiful Florence ... I am almost wild with the joy of living and seeing and being healthy in this air—saturated with the beauty of the past and present." For several days they combed the galleries and museums, strolled along the Arno, experienced some of the simple joys of travel, and recaptured the life of their marriage.

By April they were back at the Mote and reunited with their children. Will soon left for America, and Queen once again settled into the routines of the country house. But within three months word came that Ightham Mote had been sold to Thomas Colyer-Ferguson and the Palmers were given six months to find other suitable lodgings. Queen was heartbroken.

The great old house, however, would still foster one more treasure for Queen's safekeeping: a beautiful work of art.

Portrait of a Lady

During the summers of 1887 and 1888, while the Palmer women were enjoying garden picnics and stargazing at the Mote, John Singer Sargent was afoot in the Thames valley making a name for himself as a painter of landscapes and portraits of distinguished people. At thirty-one years of age, Sargent was trying to break into a field already crowded with honored and excellent artists. Queen Victoria's painters, as they were known, catered to popular tastes, pleased the royal court, and dominated the tastes of the Royal Academy, Britain's institution for training and exhibiting artists since the days of Sir Joshua Reynolds. Any artist who wished to be honored in such a fashion had to have singular gifts, dogged persistence, and some lucky breaks. Sargent tended to have all three.

He was born in Florence, Italy, in 1856 to American parents, Dr. FitzWilliam Sargent and his wife, Mary Newbold Singer. Sargent's father, a promising New England physician, had been uprooted by his ambitious wife and encouraged into a life of travel, principally among the cultural spots of Europe. They were part of that generation who never really found

John Singer Sargent, circa 1920. (Public domain)

a home, except among the distinguished and noble families of the Continent, with whom they stayed only briefly. For the first eighteen years of his life, John Sargent lived a transient life with his parents, first in Italy, then Switzerland, France, and Germany.

John spoke four languages fluently by his early twenties and played the piano with expertise. His mother was a competent watercolorist and she often encouraged her talented son to sketch and draw from early on. His talent was noted as a very young man. His early drawing skills were noted by his mentors and enabled him to enter one art school after another, first in Florence and later in Dresden and Berlin.

In 1874, the young Sargent studied in the Paris studio of Carolus-Duran. During his Paris years the maturing Sargent elicited praise from his teachers and his fellow students. His facility with drawing, particularly the human figure, was exceptional, as was his use of color and chiaroscuro. But France, like England, was a difficult place for a beginning painter to gain notice, let alone make a living.

By the time he arrived in England in 1886, he had begun to mix portrait painting with landscape. He experimented with Impressionism, then gaining much vogue in Europe. With Henry James and a few other artists, he toured the patrician haunts of London's environs, gaining experience in both outdoor and indoor scenes. "He is more intelligent about artistic things," James said of him, "than all the other painters here rolled together."[1]

By this time Sargent met and exceeded the goals of formal portraiture, which was to make his subjects nobler and more assured than they were in reality. Since the days of Romney, Gainsborough, Joshua Reynolds, and Thomas Lawrence, the formal portrait formed an important segment of British painting. To these giants of the art, Sargent added a few more important features. He had acute powers of observation that enabled him to capture the inner light of his sitters, and coupled with a bravura style and flourish, he could make a painting appear to be strikingly alive. His subjects often feared sitting for him because they knew he might expose an aspect of their personality they wished to hide. But Sargent was not merciless. He delicately walked the fine line between offending his subjects and presenting them as they were.

Sargent became eclectic in his choice of portrait subjects. Although he tended to gather at the houses of the affluent and famous, he was just as easily comfortable painting the portrait of a middle-class family. He often chose children or teenagers as subjects. He liked their spontaneity and naiveté, especially in contrast to the stuffiness of his other subjects. His technical skill and high standards demanded that the subject pose through numerous sittings. Forty sittings were common. The problem for a child or a teenager to remain relatively still posed many problems.

To get them to relax, he dashed between the piano and the easel, frequently with a cigar smoldering in the ashtray or with one sprouting from the side of his mouth. But too often, nothing helped relieve the boredom of his sitters. They stare awkwardly at the viewer, imprisoned.

Sargent was an imposing figure, standing over six feet tall with bristly dark hair and beard. A friend described him as a "curiously inarticulate man. He used to splutter and gasp, almost growl with the strain of trying to express himself."[2] But he could be the most agreeable of companions, inviting friends and family members to join him on his artistic forays around the countryside. However, at the easel he could be surly and demanding as he struggled with problems of representation. He directed most of the phases of the painting process, selecting costumes and settings for sitters and setting the tone of the work environment.

From their first meeting in 1887, when the Carrs introduced Sargent to Queen Palmer, there seemed good chemistry between the artist and Mrs. Palmer. In 1889, Sargent painted a portrait of Alma Strettel, perhaps at the Mote. That summer he painted *A Game Of Bowls* on the Mote lawn. He soon entered negotiations with Queen for a formal portrait of the Palmers. But who exactly would sit for the final painting? Queen alone? Queen and her three daughters? One of the daughters? Or two, or all three?

It is a credit to Queen that she gave that honor to her eldest daughter, Elsie. She could have stolen the spotlight for herself, but instead selected her daughter for immortality. In the summer of 1889, Elsie was sixteen years old with wistful, languid eyes and a trace of nobility shining through her awkward teen demeanor. She spoke with a distinctly English accent, as did her sisters, Dorothy and Marjory. Sargent liked her as a subject from the start. Her face was subtly tragic; her eyes were as dynamic and unusual as he had ever seen. Her right eye was a good sixteenth of an inch lower than her left eye, giving her an hypnotic and unsettling stare.

Sargent had a customary process for beginning and completing any final painting. He first had to get a feel for the atmosphere in which to paint his subject. Walking carefully through the seventy rooms of the Mote, he immediately sensed its musty medieval quality. He also liked the ghost story attached to its history, and he tumbled these features over in his mind. His final decision would come later, but his initial feelings and perceptions were formed quite early in the process.

By August he could begin the preliminary studies of Elsie, which he did in pencil, and pen and ink sketches. He also did an oil sketch of Elsie while she stood in the garden of the Mote. It was unusual for Sargent to do much preliminary work before beginning the final painting, which demonstrates how much attention he was giving to Elsie's portrait.

Elsie was not the most compliant of sitters. It may have been teen angst or feeling that she was being pushed into the commission by her mother. More often than not her expression seems to be telling Sargent: "Can't we get this over quickly." But Elsie was not an angry child. On the contrary, she had the most agreeable personality, often shrugging off problems and bearing up under her present misery.

In addition to the selection of the actual setting, the choice of dress was also important. The color, texture, and style had to be agreeable with the setting. For Elsie's portrait, Sargent and Queen selected a satin, crème white, accordion-pleated dress in agreement with the current aesthetic movement, which favored looser and more free-flowing garments than in the past. A family heirloom, a broach chosen by Queen, complemented her neckline.

At this stage in his career, the artist was aware of the concept of the "new woman" and he wished to portray Elsie in that context. In the late nineteenth century this image began to emerge in the arts, particularly in portraiture. This image discarded the notion that females were passive and unassertive and promoted the idea they engaged in new freedoms. Instead of women dependent on men as depicted in many pre-Civil War illustrations, they would assert themselves in bold new ways. The intelligent, vital, and mentally engaged "new woman" emerged in the arts and culture.[3] He had demonstrated this awareness in several previous paintings, most notably in his daring *Madam X* of 1884. Although Elsie was sixteen turning seventeen, she, in Sargent's mind, enjoyed the same freedoms as her older contemporaries.

In late October Sargent finally chose the setting for his subject: the passageway that led to the Gothic Tudor chapel; Elsie would sit on a bench with a linen fold screen directly behind her. On her seventeenth birthday, October 30, Sargent had her sit in this position on the bench. He prepared his paints and palette and went to work. Nervously puffing his cigar, he deftly drove his brush over the canvas, trusting his skills and his instincts. A wooden Elsie stared blankly back at him, her eyes drifting into a daydream.

Sargent had chosen the passageway for its dark medieval quality and for the pattern on the carved screen background. The light was brighter than the chapel itself. Since electricity was not yet introduced to the Mote, Sargent had to work strictly by daylight. In the often-dark English winters, the absence of light became a problem. More often than not, he packed up the picture and worked on it at his Tite Street studio in London.

In her diary, Elsie recorded the often-painstaking steps in the process of the finished painting:

> November 1, 1889: "I was sketched most of the morning." November 5: "Mr. Sargent arrived for dinner." December 1: "Time strangely passed since I last wrote. Hardly doing anything but sitting still with my hands folded in my lap having my portrait painted ... The weather very dark, so Mr. Sargent not able to finish me after all my sitting ..."

Although it is not known how many sittings Sargent required for the finished painting, it is apparent how laborious the task became. It took the artist over a year to complete the work. Over the course of that time, there were pleasant distractions. Alice Carr, in her *Reminiscences*, depicts a mild December day in late 1889 when Queen held a party out on the lawn. The author of the Egoist, George Meredith, and Henry James were both there, recalled Mrs. Carr. "Sargent was already staying at the house, for he was busy painting Mrs. Palmer's little daughter. It was during this visit to the Mote that Sargent was struck with the possibility of painting a picture of us as we played bowls on the big green lawn. So he sketched us all as we stooped in various attitudes, and afterwards he worked the results into one of his best pictures."[4]

It was common for Sargent to work on several pictures at one time, and this occurred with Elsie's portrait. In early 1890, he left for an extended trip to America, leaving the portrait on the easel at his London studio. In the meantime, the Palmers were eyeing a move to nearby Blackdown in Sussex. The family left their "beloved Mote" in late March 1890. Elsie sat down under the same little fir tree looking across the lake and the house that she had witnessed on her first day there in 1887. Blackdown was famous as the home of Alfred, Lord Tennyson, and evidently there was some brief connection between the Palmers and the honored poet, for his grandson, Sir Charles Tennyson, mentioned Elsie and her sisters as playmates at Blackdown.

The Palmers stayed at Blackdown until September, when they moved temporarily to London. Continuing their gypsy-like movements, they finally settled in Oak Cottage in Frant, just across the Kent border in Sussex, in October 1890. Sargent had returned from America by this time and was eager to resume his painting schedule. But a letter from his sister, Emily, to a friend suggests that the artist was encountering great difficulty with Elsie's portrait. "He [Sargent] wants dreadfully to come to Spain in the autumn but Elsie Palmer's unfinished portrait is weighing very much on his mind."[5] What troubled Sargent so much about the portrait? Was it getting Elsie's personality just right? The lighting? In an undated letter, Sargent wrote to Queen Palmer: "Elsie's picture hasn't yet come ... but I hope for wonders to be accomplished tomorrow morning. So please come with Elsie ... and we will see what we can do—with the hair if not with the picture." Since Sargent was fastidious with details, getting the correct appearance of Elsie's hair must have been concerning him in the final stages of the painting.

On November 18, 1890, Queen took Elsie to Sargent's studio on Tite Street, where Elsie remarked about "the wonderful change [in the portrait] since the last time I saw it." Two days later she commented: "Sat for the portrait all morning and after lunch, until time for music." She and Sargent's sister, Violet, had dinner together. On November 21, she sat "all morning" for the painting, and the following day she remarked that Sargent's portrait of Ellen Terry as Lady Macbeth was on the easel next to her.

After much angst and some final touch ups, the picture, known initially as "The Young Lady in White," was finally completed in December 1890. Sargent signed it in black in the lower right, "John S. Sargent," bringing to a close a difficult phase in the painting before it began its next one: its exhibition and critical reception.

The New Gallery was opened in London in 1888 by J. Comyn's Carr and Charles Halle. After the closing of the troubled Grosvenor Gallery, Carr transferred many of the paintings to the New Gallery at 121 Regent Street. Many established and aspiring artists exhibited their work there, including Burne-Jones, Lord Leighton, Alma-Tadema, and William Holman Hunt.

By 1891, and exhibition of Elsie's portrait, the New Gallery had become a Mecca for noted artists and interested buyers.

The *Portrait of Miss Elsie Palmer* was first exhibited beginning April 1891 and drew immediate criticism and much attention. Queen and her daughters attended the opening and later Will Palmer visited the gallery when he came to London. The general had remained close to the children in the last two years. A month before the opening at the New Gallery, Queen and Elsie had enjoyed a whirlwind trip to Paris, and late in 1891 it was Will's turn: he accompanied Elsie on a rail journey through the Swiss Alps.

Attendees at the exhibition also included the Strettel sisters,

Peter Harrison. Pencil sketch by John Singer Sargent, circa 1910. (Public domain)

Alma and Alice, along with Alma's new husband. In 1890, Alma married the painter Peter Harrison in a brief ceremony in London. The Harrisons and Carrs remained close through the years, often touring with Sargent on his many painting trips to the Continent.

Elsie, now eighteen, was thrilled by the painting and thanked Sargent in a letter to that effect. It was the beginning of a lifelong friendship between the Palmer children and the famed portraitist. Critics praised Sargent for his bold technique and daring brushwork and were unanimous in their concentration on Elsie's mesmerizing gaze. A reviewer for the *Times* cited the portrait's "merciless analysis of character."[6] But perhaps the most pointed criticism came from a critic for the *Magazine of Art*, who commented on the way the sitter "gazes straight out of the canvas at the spectator with an extraordinary, almost crazy, intensity of life in her wide-open brown eyes."[7]

The "extraordinary, almost crazy, intensity of life" may account for the subdued fury in the face. The many preliminary drawings, the number of sittings, and the anguish over the wrong pose became ways for Sargent to explore the deeper personality of Elsie Palmer, resulting in a picture of unusual force and restrained energy. Sargent experimented in the painting with the slight "titling pose," which employed two perspectives and exaggerated the way Elsie's figure is viewed by the spectator. If she were to stand up, the exaggeration would be evident.

Sargent used many conjurers' tricks in his portraits, "sleights of hand, odd angles, and abrupt foreshortenings to intensify the illusion of reality," noted the critic Richard Ormond. In standing poses, his subjects were often elongated to accentuate the figures of the young

Portrait of Miss Elsie Palmer *by John Singer Sargent, 1889-1890. Oil on canvas. One of the great American portraits of the nineteenth century. Courtesy of the Colorado Springs Fine Arts Center.*

women, enabling them to appear elegant, poised, and alert.[8] In his Elsie portrait, the sitting pose allowed a slight elongation to her form. Elsie was not that tall, but Sargent took liberties for effect.

From a distance the painting appears smoothly realistic and polished. But upon closer inspection the viewer can see a network of impressionistic brushstrokes. Sargent's certainty of touch becomes evident in the way he strokes in the textures of the satin dress and Elsie's hair and skin.

But beyond her regal pose and maidenly reserve, it is Elsie's facial expression and haunting eyes that stay with the viewer, revealing an unusually sensitive young woman who looks beyond the appearance of things into the mysteries of our deeper selves.

A Victorian gathering of Queen, her daughters, friends and staff possibly at Oak Cottage in England, 1893. Elsie is in the white dress and coat. Dorothy is sixth from the left, then Queen, and Marjory. Courtesy of the Starsmore Center for Local History, Colorado Springs Pioneers Museum.

The portrait remained with Queen in England and became a provocative conversation piece for visitors. She never lost sight of the importance of schooling in her daughters' lives. Living close to London, she often took her daughters into the great city, sometimes to shop on Bond and Regent Street, and more often than not to wander the museums and galleries. They rode the omnibus, walked in the parks, and watched the crowds ebb and flow around Trafalgar Square on the Strand.

Every opportunity became a teaching moment. She was concerned that because of her genteel and gracious lifestyle, the girls might not understand the misery of other people. Although she did not spend time in the East End or other dangerous places, she often pointed out how the other half lived. Elsie, Dorothy, and Marjory never forgot their tutelage in the life of the streets. Although Florence was more sunny and Paris more chic, London seemed the best place for an education for her children, providing more fullness, more drama, more concentration of life than any other place. London possessed the extremes that Glen Eyrie did not: wealth and poverty, beauty and ugliness, raw power and quiet charm, the whole madman pace of a modern urban culture.

The girls were maturing so quickly! As the decade of the 1890s opened, Dorothy, called Dos, and Marjory were about to enter their teens, and Elsie was on the verge of twenty. Queen took satisfaction in knowing she had done the best for them and provided them with the bedrock virtues to live the rest of their lives. In the summer of 1893, Queen took her daughters to Scotland, where for several weeks they toured Edinburgh, the lochs, and the highlands. A local resident taught the girls how to skip stones on the water. By the seashore, they went barefoot in the sand and picked stones off the shingle beaches. Promptly at four, Queen served them tea, and they read books like Dickens's Dombey and Son. In Edinburgh they learned to pick out plaids and watched the changing of the guard at the castle. "We saw some soldiers with very pretty kilts," noted Dorothy.[9] All too soon, the holiday was over and they returned in good spirits to Sussex.

But Queen was not well, as even minor stresses fatigued her. She often took to her bed and stayed for days on end. The governess, Anna, kept the children busy by writing in their journals and completing their lessons. The girls wrote Will of their adventures. Over the years Queen had written several farewell notes to her children. She knew it was time for Elsie to be with her father, so in early 1894 she gave Elsie her blessing to be with Will in Glen Eyrie.

Nomads

With the official closing of the American frontier in 1890, Will Palmer lost the part of the spirit of the great West that he had gained in the 1860s and '70s, rambling around the Southwest and establishing his baby railroad in Colorado. But even though the West had been sectioned and mapped, there were still vast wild spaces to be explored. The untamed Rockies rose above the city he had founded, now closing in on twelve thousand residents. The land north to the Palmer Ridge Divide was largely unsettled, and the area known as the Pinery was yielding wood for the rising structures in town. To the east, sprawling ranches were extending deep into the homes of buffalo and pronghorn antelope. South of Cheyenne Mountain, the land sloped away to Pueblo, now a major center of coal production and a hub in railroad commerce. Beyond the extent of one's vision, far to the north and east, there were still large tracts of uninhabited prairie, some in stubble and stone, and others in tall, green, knee-high grasses.

Will was surprised that the West itself had suddenly found its way into popular culture. Legends of gunslingers, cowpokes, outlaws, bloodletters, shady women, and devious railroad men found their way into a plethora of dime novels and cheap journals. Tombstone, Dodge City, and Deadwood made reputations that would make the residents of Colorado Springs shudder in disbelief.

And from all the chatter, a substantial myth had emerged—

among writers, illustrators, and politicians, one that would sustain the western genre into the next century. The West according to the myth held the moral cure for the disease affecting the American male population. It turned ordinary weaklings into men of strength and stature, and it provided independence from a life of boredom and indolence. Books were being written testifying to the reality of the myth. One, by a politician turned cowboy by the name of Theodore Roosevelt, titled *Ranch Life and the Hunting Trail*, popularized the myth even more. "I would strongly recommend," a burly Roosevelt said to a friend, "for a good healthy experience that some of our golden youth go west and try a short course in riding bucking ponies."[1] Even respected journals like *Harper's Weekly* and *Harper's Monthly* featured western themes and maintained the idea that the Old West was not dead—it was only napping. They hired illustrators such as Frederic Remington to dispense the legends with drama and accuracy. General William Jackson Palmer, self-made and self-

View of the Colorado Avenue bridge, 1900, with Pikes Peak in the distance. Courtesy of the Starsmore Center for Local History, Colorado Springs Pioneers Museum.

deprecating to a fault, embodied the myth, and although he probably would not admit it, enjoyed the role.

Palmer's little hamlet was increasing in modernization and sophistication. Bank deposits had escalated five times. A Board of Trade had been established to govern commerce. Five railroads traveled along the Monument Creek route. Electric streetcars replaced horse-drawn vehicles. New hotels—the Alamo, the Alta Vista, and the Elk—were opening to give the Antlers competition. A seventeen-mile carriage road had been cut through the forested slopes of Pikes Peak.[2]

But nearby Colorado City refused to grow up with its neighbor. It still retained its tough image, packing in its share of saloons and shady dens and welcoming new residents who thought Colorado Springs was too boring. Notorious watering holes like the Crystal Palace thrived. Jesse James's killer, Bob Ford, roosted here and the law—such as it was—left him alone.

Will and Queen Palmer's glen, however, was still wild and primitive in its own way, providing solace and an antidote to both the plusses and evils of civilization. The seventeen-room house still stood proudly among the rock outcroppings under the fir and pine trees. John Blair's gardens ringed the house and a lawn had been added so that Will Palmer and his guests could relax in big chairs on summer evenings and watch the hawks circle above. He had brought in some eastern furnishings so that the interior was downright fashionable for a western home. In 1883, Palmer had begun a serious planting program around the house, and now, seven years later, it was full of maturing grapevines plus peach, apricot, and nectarine trees. He also had created a vast network of irrigation and sprinkler systems.[3] It was Palmer's wish that the entire eastern slope of the Rocky Mountains facing Colorado Springs be maintained as a forest preserve.

In 1891, a seismic shift occurred that changed the fortunes of Colorado Springs. Gold was discovered in Cripple Creek, just eighteen miles over the mountains from the center of town. Not since the great Leadville boom of the 1880s had a strike excited the hearts and minds of Colorado prospectors and developers alike. Within months, gold production from the mines soared, increasing from $2 million worth in 1893 to $10 million in 1897. By 1900, the worth had doubled. Bank deposits increased nine times. The population began soaring. The Springs could count fifty millionaires as a result of the Cripple Creek gold strike, and along Tejon Street four hundred and twenty mining companies were bustling with activity.

The second Antlers Hotel constructed in 1898. Courtesy of the Starsmore Center for Local History, Colorado Springs Pioneers Museum.

One of the most prominent new millionaires was the unimaginative, forty-five-year-old, silver-haired bachelor, Winfield Scott Stratton, whom Will Palmer came to regard with disdain. In 1893, Stratton discovered a twenty-seven foot vein of gold that became the Independence Mine in Cripple Creek. Within weeks the impoverished Stratton, who lived on three dollars a day, was showered with enormous wealth that suddenly inflated his wage to $3,000 per day. But as Stratton's reputation grew, Will looked the other way, refusing to believe that this upstart ex-carpenter could challenge him for distinction among the good folks of Colorado Springs.[4]

Soon, two rival camps developed: those allied with General Palmer who wished to keep the refinement and dignity of their town alive, and those of the gold-seeking crowd, who sought to turn it into a hell-raising, boom or bust outpost. Besides, the two men made their wealth in distinctly different ways. Palmer could claim that he made his through painstaking, labored, and scrupulous means, while Stratton was forced to admit he literally stumbled into a goldmine. With their backgrounds and personalities so different, it is no wonder that the two rarely if ever acknowledged one another.

Stratton's ten-year legacy as Colorado's "Midas of the Rockies," in the words of writer Frank Waters, came to an end in 1902. In that time he had managed to squander a third of his fortune on several exploratory trips to Cripple Creek to find more gold deposits and on a modern trolley system; the rest was given away frivolously to anyone with his hand out. A prospector and speculator to the end, he died of acute alcoholism at the age of fifty-four.

Dignitaries, Presidents, and Presidential hopefuls were always welcome in Colorado Springs. These included the New York banker and railroad man, George Peabody, and the sitting President, Benjamin Harrison. Harrison was particularly in favor because of his distinguished Civil War record and his staunch Republican values. When Grover Cleveland, a Democrat, became president in 1893, Palmer did not give him the same support. For one thing, Cleveland avoided Civil War service by paying a Polish immigrant $150 to serve in his place. Such a move was legal, but for Palmer it signaled a significant character flaw.

In his late fifties, Will enjoyed the routines at Glen Eyrie and attended the civic events in Colorado Springs, life activities that he could not indulge in as a busy entrepreneur and railroad president. His mornings were usually crowded with reading and maintaining a steady stream of correspondence. Some letters were written to national figures, others to prominent state officials. His library revealed the range of his tastes and interests, from Dickens's *Our Mutual Friend* and *Bleak House* to James Whistler's *The Gentle Art of*

Making Enemies, and the *Poems of George Herbert*.

In the afternoon, he might take a horse for a jog in Garden of the Gods. It was a way he kept in touch with the land he had loved for nearly a quarter of a century and one that he had difficulty leaving even for a short time. He chose an Irish thoroughbred or a western quarter horse for the occasion. One of his Great Danes might accompany him as he made his way out the road to the gate and turned south along the narrow path to the Garden.

The Garden prompted many different responses from many diverse people, but for Palmer it remained a wild, pristine place near the heart of town, and one that resisted civilization fast encroaching on the Rockies. Amid the piñon and juniper and under the shadow of

Palmer and Dorothy near the stone wall at Glen Eyrie, circa 1895. Courtesy of the Starsmore Center for Local History, Colorado Springs Pioneers Museum.

Pikes Peak he could lose himself in the many trails twisting through the Garden. The owner, Charles Perkins, gave him special permission to wander where he liked. On warm summer days, when the sun lingered far into the evening, he dismounted on a ridge and simply listened to the silence.

He divided his days between Glen Eyrie and his new hobby, riding in his designer train named the Nomad. Built in 1878, the car measured fifty feet in length by eight in width and was part of a three-car train. The first car contained a kitchen and berths for the crew; the second was a sleeping car; the last car was Palmer's private, luxurious suite on wheels, complete with steam heat, plush red upholstery, and mahogany furniture. It also contained a business room, full bed, and a lavatory; a glassed-in observatory at the rear held gauges and a speed meter. In the Nomad, Palmer traveled around the country visiting friends and business connections.

When Elsie Palmer arrived in New York in early 1894, Will was there with his train fully prepped for their enjoyment. After a ten-year hiatus from Colorado, Elsie was thrilled to be once again in her father's company and to see America from his posh train. Jostling along at a leisurely pace, the train headed along the eastern seaboard and through the south. In her diary Elsie mentions stops at homes of prominent families, including the Carnegies and the Vanderbilts. The train then headed west to Texas, New Mexico, and finally Colorado Springs, where they were greeted by a crowd of well-wishers. A crew shunted the Nomad onto a spur line near the depot.

At Glen Eyrie, Elsie was showered with attention and affection by the staff. She spent her days reminiscing and taking walks in the garden. Notable citizens stopped by, including the Gilpins, who inquired about Queen and Elsie's sisters in England. Too soon, the Nomad whisked her and her father north through Wyoming and out to the Pacific Northwest. By September she had boarded a ship bound for England.

Upon her return to Oak Cottage, Elsie found that Queen Palmer's condition had worsened. Queen's doctors had her confined much of the time to her bed and had the staff prevent the children from seeing her suffer. Elsie and Dorothy sent her notes and waited for

*Elsie Palmer circa 1892. Courtesy of the Starsmore Center
for Local History, Colorado Springs Pioneers Museum.*

her written reply. Through the autumn and early December, Queen endured sleeplessness and frequent pains in her chest. Her half-sisters arrived: Maud, Daisy, Lottie, and Helen. By Christmas the atmosphere at Oak Cottage turned grave. On Christmas day, Elsie wrote her a note: "Good morning—my own darling Motherling—I can write you now but I can't talk to you because it tires you ... we feel your presence with us every second. It's wonderful how you do that. And all your little thoughts for people's pleasure—come showering downstairs to everyone, and are kept close all the time—almost as if you were there."[5]

The following day, when she began to slip even more, Will was notified to come at once. The twelve-day journey by train and ship, combined with extreme worry, exhausted him. But it was too late. Queen Palmer, at the age of forty-four, died on the morning of December 28 with her daughters, sisters, and friends by her side. Elsie simply noted in her diary: "Mother died today. Beautiful morning, sunrise."[6]

After the funeral, Will began settling the family's financial affairs in England and, with the help of his daughters and the Harrisons, coping with the loss of his wife. On December 31, 1894, the Colorado Springs *Evening Telegraph* paid tribute to Queen in an editorial, which said in part: "No one more fully understood and answered the demands of friendship with grace and satisfaction than Mrs. Palmer, a loving, devoted, and judicious mother, a wise and charming presider over her household. Our tender sympathy goes out to those who are bereaved of her gentle guidance and beautiful presence." Other eulogies and tributes followed, focusing on her contributions to the founding and development of Colorado Springs.

Will and his three daughters arrived somberly in Colorado late in the winter of 1895, where they continued to mourn Queen's passing. A few months after Queen's death, a strange package postmarked from England arrived at Glen Eyrie. Inside was Queen's watch, given to her by General Palmer, with no return address or name of sender included.

The first six months of 1895 were a period of adjustment for Will Palmer and his daughters. Dorothy and Marjory barely knew the place, and Elsie spent her time reacquainting herself with the routines at the castle. Will's customary authoritarian habits suddenly had to be modified to accommodate his growing daughters. His military ways had not worked on Queen and they certainly were not going to work on his headstrong, twenty-two-year-old daughter, Elsie. One acquaintance that regularly visited Glen Eyrie called him "a charming tyrant. He made plans for each day and everybody fell in line. He issued orders as if we were a troop of cavalry on special exploring detail."7

Two events occurring beyond the shores of America tested Will's commitment to democratic ideals and his steadfast belief that the United States should not become an imperial power. The first involved a border dispute between Great Britain and Venezuela; the second generated much more interest and fear among Americans: the Cubans revolt against Spanish rule and the eventual run-up to the Spanish-American War. Both conflicts would involve the interpretation of the Monroe Doctrine and bring America into the forefront of world politics.

By this time General Palmer had influence both at the state level and in Washington. The year before he had received the Medal of Honor for actions in the Civil War. The medal added to his stature, giving him a platform that few in the West could equal.

The first of the conflicts exposed the general's sympathies toward Great Britain, sympathies that were perceived as anti-American by the jingoistic press. Although the Venezuela boundary question was not a major international incident, it did have resonance in the West, particularly in Colorado Springs. Two newspapers, the *El Paso County Democrat* and the *Evening Telegraph*, accused Palmer of being pro-English in the matter, a development that threatened to widen the gap between him and the residents of the town. It was a time of rising nationalism that sought to make America a global power. Writing in his own newspaper, the *Manitou Springs Journal*, Palmer stated that, "the United States has really no more right to meddle in Venezuelan boundary affairs than it has to meddle in the boundary of the Kingdom of Heaven."8

Whether it was a way of coping with his part in Queen's early death or dealing with his role as a father of three girls, Will plunged into battle against America's inexorable march toward imperialism. He maintained his firm right-wing principles of independence, personal rights, and isolationism in the world. He believed that countries were sovereign entities and as such needed to resolve their own struggles and conflicts. He remembered vividly the Civil War and the cost it took in young lives. He did not want to fight for another person's ideology or to spill American blood for the sake of a foreign country's war for independence. Although he had his supporters, such a course was to isolate him from the constituents who encouraged him and financed him early on.

It was an age when imperialism and foreign involvement were popular issues. In 1885, Josiah Strong published *Our Country*, which was to serve as a rallying cry for supporters of American interests in foreign lands. A mélange of racism, patriotism, and avarice, Strong's book promoted the idea that America's next manifest destiny lay beyond its shores. His argument was plain and strident, and although misguided, highly influential: America's right and duty was to export its way of life and form of government to strategic places around the world. Strong reasoned that the Anglo-Saxon race had been chosen by God to lead the other races and foster a higher civilization around the globe. Even after weeding out the racist and bigoted references, readers sensed the possibilities of Strong's imperialist message. By the mid-1890s, Strong's ideas had been taken up by a growing number of politicians and seekers of public office.

Eighteen ninety-six was one of those milestone years in Will Palmer's life. Colorado celebrated twenty years of statehood, the city honored its twenty-five-year existence, and General Palmer turned sixty years of age. Before those events could happen, however, fire broke out in Cripple Creek in April and threatened to engulf the entire town. With more than half the town razed and five thousand people forced out of their homes, desperate appeals for help reached Colorado Springs. Since Cripple Creek officials refused to use city funds to fight the blaze, Winfield Scott Stratton, the gold king, sent his own trainload of supplies to the stricken town. In all, Stratton spent over $50,000 of his money on food supplies and relief efforts.[9]

Despite the Cripple Creek fire, the town's festivities went on as scheduled in July and August. Tourists descended on the Garden of the Gods, Manitou Springs, and the Cave of the Winds. The general and his daughters hosted several gala parties at Glen Eyrie featuring many local and state dignitaries, including the Bells of Manitou and London and the Byers family of Denver. By now Elsie, Dorothy, and Marjory were learning how to give a party and dinner at the castle and what pleased the general and what got under his skin. Elsie took the lead, showing her teenage sisters how to set a table and stimulate conversation among the guests.

But beyond the festivities in Colorado Springs, Palmer was worried about the direction of the country. For several months, debate had raged in Congress over whether to arm Cuban insurgents in their fight against the Spanish. The controversy soon percolated through the country and was taken up by ordinary citizens. The Venezuelan dispute, which was settled in 1899, appeared tame in comparison with the present conflict that was taking place ninety miles off the American coast. Realizing that circulations, and hence profit margins, could jump with an imminent war, American newspapers and journals took up the cause.

With the unshaken belief that Americans loved an underdog, two rival newspapers sent their best reporters and illustrators into the field to build a case for American military intervention in the Cuban insurrection. William Randolph Hearst's *New York Journal* and Joseph Pulitzer's *World* battled for dominance in the largely savage arena of New York publishing. Both newspapers wished to extend the sensationalism of Civil War journalism and reach new audiences among arriving immigrants unfamiliar with the customs of America. Pulitzer even remarked that, "he rather liked the idea of a war—not a big one—but one which arouse interest and let us gauge the reflex in circulation figures."[10]

At the end of 1896, Hearst offered the flamboyant reporter, Richard Harding Davis, three thousand dollars plus all expenses for a month's reporting from Cuba. Dressed in British khaki and sporting a revolver and field glasses, the intrepid Davis headed for Cuba along with illustrator Frederic Remington. Although their assignment was thwarted by the lack of a seaworthy boat, they tried again in early 1897 with an interpreter and several staff reporters. The team got as far as Matanzas, a province between Havana and Santa Clara. With few signs of a rebellion, a disgruntled Remington cabled William Hearst:

"Everything is quiet. There is no trouble here. There will be no war. I wish to return. Remington." Hearst's now famous reply ran: "Please remain. You furnish the pictures, I'll furnish the war." The source of this exchange was *Journal* reporter James Creelman. The cable has never been corroborated and writing a decade later, Hearst himself dismissed it as "clotted nonsense." He additionally denounced the existence of such a cable and for his role in creating the Spanish-American War. But fabricated or not, the telegram remains central to Hearst's legacy in shaping the eventual war with Spain.[11]

Davis continued to report from the Spanish-ruled island. A brilliant article came from his sojourn among the Cuban rebels, "The Death of Rodriquez," which did much to inflame public opinion back home in America. Told in deadpan reportorial style, the story relates how a Cuban rebel captured in a skirmish is publicly executed by firing squad. As Davis witnessed the event he wrote: "As I looked back, the figure of a young Cuban, who was no longer a part of the world of Santa Clara, was asleep in the wet grass, with his motionless arms still tightly bound about him, with the scapular twisted awry about his face, and the blood from his breast sinking into the soil he had tried to free."[12]

Hearst was delighted with the story and found it perfect copy for the evening news. Richard Harding Davis became an overnight sensation and Hearst raised his wages accordingly. He eventually sought the services of Stephen Crane, famed author of *The Red Badge of Courage*, who, like Davis, turned his experiences in Cuba into front-page news.

As both newspapers' circulation soared and American public opinion swerved toward the Cuban militants, Will Palmer remained unmoved by the hysteria. From his desk at Glen Eyrie, he wrote numerous letters and public statements opposing American intervention in Cuba. It helped that the newly elected U.S. president, William McKinley, also voiced caution in the Cuban matter. McKinley, like Palmer, fought in the Civil War and was similarly reluctant to rush to war on the Cubans' behalf.

Palmer knew he was in a minority, both on the question of intervention in Cuba and on America's global ambitions. The European powers, particularly Germany and Great Britain, were in the process of increasing the sizes of their navies. Many in Congress felt that America had come of age after the Civil War and with its industrial might was ready to take its rightful place among the leading powers in the world. Perhaps the most vocal was Massachusetts Senator Henry Cabot Lodge who argued that intervention in Cuba was America's duty: "The sympathies of the American people, generous, liberty-loving ... are with the Cubans in their struggle for freedom. I believe our people would welcome any action on the part of the United States to put an end to the terrible state of things existing there. We can stop it. We can stop it peacefully ..."[13]

The Cuban crisis exposed many of Palmer's most cherished political and social beliefs. He believed that the current immigration problem was sufficiently complex "without introducing another discordant element." Additionally, he insisted that "the democratic institutions of the United States were already endangered by attempting to stretch them over too wide a surface," and that the United States had no right to intervene in Cuba if it did not intend to annex it or remain there to govern it. One of his central ideas was that the republican form of government was as ineffective as a dictatorship; he seriously began to mistrust the health of democratic governments. He went one step further in saying he was taking "a wait and see" attitude toward democracy, and that he was hopeful at times about it and discouraged by it at others. "It is quite true," he wrote "that I don't care for the form as such ... The great masses of the people would be better off if directed and controlled by a small body of highly-equipped men." What he meant by "highly equipped," Palmer did not elaborate.[14]

Palmer displayed all the attributes of an isolationist who favored limited involvement in international disputes, who sought no additional territories outside the United States, and who spent only such capital for the good of the citizens of the country.[15]

His religious views had undergone a serious shift as well. His western experiences, his international travel, and his railroad dealings had eroded his firm belief in Quaker values. He now considered agnosticism "almost a condition precedent to belief, and that all other men than agnostics are more liable than they to cynicism. Only people who wait for the proof are the real disciples of belief, and are free in a comparative sense from the risk of, what shall we call them, intellectual washouts.[16]

After the sinking of the USS *Maine* and the killing of 260 of its crew in Havana Harbor on February 15, 1898, the efforts of the sensationalist press switched into overdrive. Although Spain denied any involvement in the explosion and although investigations were underway, the press seized the moment. Lurid tales of atrocities filled the front pages as editors sent reporters scurrying into the field to report from the scene. Cable charges for a story ran $8,000, but since money was not an issue, newspapers gladly paid the bill. Hearst's and Pulitzer's newspaper circulation figures climbed dizzily as the crisis unfolded day by day in Cuba. Larger and larger headline type was employed to lure readers' attention, until letters four inches high and printed in red dominated the front pages. Reporters' stories had to match the headlines. One reporter wondered if "there was some factory out there for faking war news."[17]

As the investigation into the cause of the explosion continued, Palmer urged restraint. He was willing to wait until the investigation revealed a cause, but asserted that he "was ready to jump on [Spain] if our divers show that [it] had lied."[18] Palmer at this point was not totally against war with Spain, but only on the condition that it had caused the sinking of the *Maine*. Only acting to protect America's interests was a war justified in his mind. He did not react when the U.S. Ambassador to Great Britain, John Hay, characterized the conflict "as a splendid little war ... favored by fortune that loves the brave." [19]

During the late spring of 1898, as Congress and the President moved ever closer to the brink of war with Spain, Palmer created and sent a petition to his fellow Union officer and President, William McKinley. It partially said that, "we earnestly hope that in behalf of justice, humanity, and our permanent national welfare the United States will continue to refrain from hostile intervention in Cuba. A false step at this time may bring war, and it is possible for victory by begetting a willingness to interfere in the affairs of other nations, to produce results that might be worse than defeat."[20] McKinley was being pressured from both sides of his party. The hawks, led by Under Secretary of the Navy Theodore Roosevelt, Henry Cabot Lodge, and former Confederate General Fitzhugh Lee pressed for war. Non-interventionists and pacifists, both inside the Republican and Democratic parties were also in abundance.

On April 11, 1898, after peace initiatives with Spain had stalled, President McKinley delivered his war message to Congress. A week later Congress adopted a war resolution, which declared in part that the U.S. would respect Cuban independence from Spain and that Spanish armed forces needed to evacuate the island. From that point the gears of war started grinding. McKinley called up 125,000 volunteers for active service, and the Pacific fleet sailed to the Philippines to engage the Spanish at Manila Bay. By late June and early July, American ground forces landed in Cuba and began assaulting the entrenched Spanish batteries located on the heights.

The fighting in Cuba and the Philippines during the summer months of 1898, at least as perceived by the American newspapers, was a glorious, short and "splendid little war" that united the country, proved our military might, and dispelled any notion that America was a backwater, provincial nation still reeling from the effects of its Civil War. Of course the man who championed these values of expansionism and military preparedness was Theodore Roosevelt, who emerged from the Spanish-American War as a national hero, and anyone who questioned that claim just had to ask him. Palmer admired Roosevelt's personality more than he did his policies. Although Roosevelt's pompous strut, toothy grin, and bullying tone aggravated Palmer, he did admire his handling of America's precious natural resources and national parks.

One feature that nettled Palmer about Roosevelt was his open campaign to win the Medal of Honor, which Roosevelt thought he deserved for gallantry during the battles of Kettle Hill and San Juan Hill in early July 1898. He wrote letters to congressmen citing his actions and urged fellow Rough Riders to do the same. Roosevelt later recalled his "crowded hour" during the battle to take the heights: how he rallied his men wearing a blue polka-dot scarf dangling backward from his hat; how on horseback he urged his men up San Juan Hill while Spanish bullets perforated the leaves and sounded like "the ripping of a silk dress"; how he reached the wire fence near the top of the hill, turned his horse loose and fought the remaining way on foot; how, despite numerous Rough Rider casualties, his men yelled and cheered as they drove the Spanish soldiers from their positions on the summit; and how Roosevelt, with "the wolf rising in his heart," stormed and secured the top of the hill for the advancing American forces. "San Juan was the great day of my life," he wrote. Fame and adulation quickly followed, and Teddy felt he deserved the Medal of Honor for his valor in Cuba.[21]

Palmer hated self-promotion and never would have considered lobbying for the Medal of Honor on his own behalf. However, the route to his being awarded the medal proved to be of interest. In January of 1893, six former high-ranking officers of the Fifteenth Pennsylvania Cavalry petitioned the War Department to award Palmer the Medal of Honor for his work as a spy in Virginia after the Battle of Antietam. In August the same year, the War Department replied that Palmer's "services as specified do not seem to constitute the conscious gallantry in action for which medals are issued."[22] The department was empathic that, despite Palmer's heroics as a spy, his actions did not happen on the field of battle, and that is what characterized the ultimate criteria for the award. The following month another petition was sent to the War Department that recounted General Palmer's actions during the battle at Red Hill, Alabama. The petition cited that General Palmer's command took "ninety-five prisoners, one hundred and twenty horses and one piece of artillery, while losing only one man in the process."[23] Five months later, in early 1894, the War Department notified Palmer that he had been awarded the Medal of Honor. Palmer immediately wrote back asking for the names of the men who helped him win the award. "I should like to thank these unknown friends for their kind offices," he said.[24]

A gratified and humble Palmer always believed that his unit, as much as he, deserved the award. Later, he wrote the introduction to the history of the Fifteenth Pennsylvania Cavalry, in which he said in part: "It was a great and pure cause for which they fought,

The Palmer sisters, circa 1900, on the terrace of Glen Eyrie. Marjory, Elsie, Dorothy, left to right. Courtesy of the Starsmore Center for Local History, Colorado Springs Pioneers Museum.

and if war is ever justifiable, their consciences are clear that this one was so. I am proud to have commanded and to have since retained the respect and confidence of such a body of men goes without saying."[25]

Largely due to his own efforts to win the medal and his cold relationship with the Secretary of War, Roosevelt was initially denied the nation's highest military award. Not until 2001—over a hundred years after the battle—was he awarded the Medal of Honor. The Spanish-American War was substantially over by the end of July 1898, when Spain requested peace terms. Only three months in duration, the war settled many issues fomenting in American foreign policy, a critical one being expansionism in the Pacific with the annexation of Hawaii and the capture of the Philippines. Other principles that Palmer held dear would be tested in the coming years.

The war was over for the country, but for Theodore Roosevelt the journey to the White House was just beginning.

If Will Palmer had any intention of remarrying as the century closed, he made no mention of it to those around him. Although he had the opportunity, he never really pursued a romantic relationship with a woman. Five years after Queen's death, he was still deeply attached to her memory.

His daughters doted on him but at the same time declared their independence. They made new friends in Colorado but their lifelong friends remained in England. They kept up regular correspondence with Alma and Peter Harrison, as well as the Carrs. Dorothy Comyns Carr, the daughter of Alice and Joseph, also became a friend and expressed interest in seeing the girls in Glen Eyrie. Whether Will offered his daughters the chance to attend college is not known, but it would seem obvious given the proximity of Colorado College to their home.

In October of 1898, fire gutted the Antlers Hotel. On an arid day with a gusty wind out of the southwest, the fire broke out in the freight depot of the Denver and Rio Grande Railroad, tore through the nearby lumberyards, and began consuming the Antlers Hotel. Townspeople turned out bearing buckets of water in an effort to prevent the fire from reaching the south wing of the hotel. The entire downtown was threatened. Fire brigades from as far away as Pueblo and Denver arrived by train to assist in dampening the fire.

Palmer was out of town at the time, but when he learned that the hotel had been lost and a $250,000 loss incurred, he immediately began plans to rebuild. By the end of 1899, work was underway. The new Antlers Hotel would have all the modern conveniences and features and once again be the showcase of the Rockies.

As the last months of the old century waned, transportation methods began changing—and

Dorothy Palmer, circa 1903. Courtesy of the Starsmore Center for Local History, Colorado Springs Pioneers Museum.

not everyone appreciated those changes. Streetcars and horse-drawn buggies still plied the main thoroughfares, as did pedestrians and bicyclists in trilbys and straw boater hats. In the mid- nineties a few stray horseless carriages appeared, but it was not until July 1899 that one was actually reported by the *Gazette*.

Its appearance caused excitement with the citizens and panic among the horses. The machine fouled the air with the new smell of a gasoline engine, as the goggle-wearing drivers honked into town, drawing crowds and the shouts of furious horsemen trying to control their mounts. This first-reported car was homemade and painted red, gold, and maroon. Built in Denver by two mechanics, it purportedly spent two days getting to the Springs. More time was spent pausing to fill up with gasoline than was enjoyed viewing the scenery.

The automobile craze affected the whole country. Even President McKinley took a ride in a spanking new Stanley Steamer at a speed of twenty miles an hour and pronounced it "thrilling." But according to the *Literary Digest* of October 1899, the assessment of its longevity was not as enthusiastic: "The ordinary horseless carriage is at present a luxury for the wealthy; and although its price will probably fall in the future, it will never, of course, come into as common a use as the bicycle."[26]

The New Glen Eyrie

Despite the new century not officially beginning until the year 1901, Palmer and everyone else got a jump on things and started celebrating at midnight, December 31, 1899. Although still guided by stringent standards of drinking alcohol, he allowed himself and his guests a glass of wine or two from his cellar stocked with German, Italian, and French wines. Champagne, of course, was uncorked for special occasions. His strict temperance ban for his city was still on the books, but he recognized the futility of enforcing such a ban. Colorado City alone had over twenty saloons and although a few drinking establishments were beginning to show up here and there in Colorado Springs, the avoidance of spirits was largely followed.

Many gloomy prophets had predicted financial ruin or military apocalypse on the eve of the twentieth century, but for the most part it was an age of buoyant optimism. A new vigor seemed to overtake the country with the second term administration of William McKinley and his irrepressible running mate, Theodore Roosevelt, who one aide dubbed "that damned cowboy" and "a madman one heartbeat away from the presidency."[1] Will's attitude toward the vice- president had slowly changed. He now viewed Roosevelt's blustery personality with a combination of humor and indifference. The war in Cuba was over and the populist tide of nineties had subsided, as a new spirit of progressivism began to gain momentum. If America could restrain its imperialist ambitions, Will maintained, it would have a glorious future.

General Palmer could point to the wretched conditions of other American cities—urban overcrowding, ineffective schools, rampant crime, political corruption, and choking pollution—and claim victory in the development of his city beneath Pikes Peak. Although it possessed the problems of any growing city, he felt that Colorado Springs had managed to avoid most of them. The air was still pure and the white-capped Rockies rose razor-sharp against the deep blue sky. Unemployment stood at roughly four percent. Crime was sporadic but kept under control by a staff of twenty officers. In all, for a town nearly thirty years old and reaching out to a variety of settlers and immigrants, it was a model of efficiency and respectability.

The new Antlers Hotel was ready for its dedication in the summer of 1901. While the old structure had Old World elegance, the new hotel was imposing and fortress-like, its massive walls used to

The Myron Stratton home and cottages, circa 1900. Courtesy of the Starsmore Center for Local History, Colorado Springs Pioneers Museum.

accommodate a plethora of modern features and many additional rooms. The British-born architect, Frederick Sterner, designed it, and like many of the buildings in Colorado, it reflected his interest in Queen Anne, early Norman, and English Gothic architecture. He was steeped in the Ruskin school, which favored the sanctity of historic styles. In front of the hotel, citizens erected a statue of Zebulon Pike, who first saw the mountain that bears his name in 1806. The statue was set to be unveiled during the festivities of August 1–3, with several distinguished orators in attendance, General Palmer and Vice President Roosevelt among them.

Roosevelt liked public speaking about as much as Palmer loathed it. Approaching sixty-five years of age, Will had never gotten used to the spotlight and considered speaking before an audience as threatening as standing before a firing squad. He liked writing speeches, but the job ended upon mounting the platform. He was still rail-thin with streaks of gray hair beginning to vine their way through his curls. His skin was leathery and red from the sun; his gray eyes were still sharp and he read with undiminished clarity. His neatly trimmed mustache gave him an aristocratic look. The years had softened his hard edges but he walked and rode a horse with military bearing. He remained authoritarian in the way he managed the household, reminding his staff that he was still the general.

Palmer was gruff and insistent, but he also displayed great kindness and sensitivity. Once while riding in the Nomad, he spotted a hobo walking by the side of the tracks. He asked one of his staff to get the man cleaned up, fed, and provide him a ride to his destination. "No one will ever know the extent of his private pension list," noted one of his household staff. "For years he kept in his employ scores of old and crippled men unable to do a day's work, simply because he knew that they needed the money."[2] He never forgot where he came from or the growl of an empty stomach.

In mid-summer 1901, George Jay Gould, the son of the noted financier, bought out General Palmer's controlling interest in the Rio Grande Western, providing Palmer with a hefty $6 million for his three hundred and forty mile railroad.[3] He gave one million dollars of that to his employees of the Rio Grande Western, a rather generous move and Palmer did it without publicity. He now had financial freedom, and coupled with income from his other Colorado properties, realized a monthly inflow of $30,000, a princely sum even in today's standards. He immediately continued his philanthropy by donating the 753 acres of Palmer Park to the city, as well as additional land for the public library, Colorado College, the Cragmor Sanitorium, and the Deaf and Blind Institute. He provided monies to enhance the natural features—trees, gardens, fountains, and parks—in downtown and outlying areas. He did all that was monetarily possible to sustain Colorado Springs in the early years of the decade and make its legacy last well into the rest of the century.

His financial windfall allowed him not only to retire worry-free, but also to begin considering expanding and enhancing his Glen Eyrie estate—something, he thought, Queen would have encouraged.

To add to the excitement of the new Antlers Hotel and General Palmer's retirement, there was also romance in the air. In the summer of 1901, Elsie Palmer had met Leopold Hamilton Myers in New York and there was already talk of engagement and marriage. But Elsie downplayed such chatter. She was never one to rush into anything, and marriage and all its constraints frightened her. Besides, she had her mother's fierce independence and was not willing to surrender it too quickly.

Leo Myers was understanding and let their romance develop without pressure. He was nineteen when he met Elsie, she was twenty-eight. He came from a distinguished family in Cambridge, England. His father, Frederick Myers, was a classical scholar and literary critic, but his main interest was the world of the paranormal and the serious investigation of the world of spiritualism. He was one of the original founders of the Society for Psychical Research in Great Britain, whose other members included a rich strata of British society including clergymen, philosophers, and university professors. His mother was Eveline Tennant Myers, a photographer of considerable talent, who maintained a studio in the Myers's home and whose work was exhibited in the National Portrait Gallery in London.

It was an age when spiritualism was in vogue. Frederick Myers always stayed above the fraud and phoniness of much of the movement, preferring instead to focus on the more scientific aspects of consciousness and brain development. He published two seminal works: *Phantasm of the Living* (1886) and *Human Personality and its Survival of Bodily Death* (1903), which influenced several important psychologists and philosophers including William James and Carl Jung. What is noteworthy about Myers's work is that he studied the full range of human experience, both the normal and paranormal, in probing the conscious and unconscious mind.

Leo Myers grew up in Leckhampton House in Cambridge, a charming country manor house whose frequent visitors included many mediums and spiritualists from across England and Scotland. As

Palmer seated in den at Glen Eyrie with one of his dogs, circa 1895.Note the jumbled collection of books in the basket next to him. Courtesy of the Starsmore Center for Local History, Colorado Springs Pioneers Museum.

a young man he attended Eton College, where he met Lottie Mellen's sons, Eric and Cyril, who were also being schooled there. Leo was often tutored by his father, both before and during his undergraduate days at Cambridge University, where he began studies in 1898. But upset by the unexpected death of his father in January 1901, he left the university and took his grieving mother to New York in hopes of easing her sorrow. There he met Elsie Palmer, and perhaps his own vulnerability led them into a sudden romance.

From the start there was compatibility and minor friction. Elsie helped soothe Leo's loss, and in turn Leo provided Elsie with a charming escort among the socialites of New York and Newport. As a worldly, vivacious, and wealthy American woman, she coaxed her suitor out of his shell and gave him confidence in the world beyond Cambridge and England. Leo provided Elsie with intelligent and witty conversation. As their relationship deepened, there was talk of marriage, but Elsie preferred to wait.

She was intrigued by Leo's mysticism. They frequently talked about communication with the deceased, and since one of each of their parents had passed away—Leo's the more recently—they took comfort in each other's beliefs of the afterlife. Elsie loved his ability to recite verse; often he would break into a conversation with a phrase from Shelley or Swinburne. Throughout their years together, they shared an abiding interest in the life of the spirit.

Elsie's eyes—the same eyes that gazed with unearthly passion from Sargent's portrait—attracted Leo from the beginning. He saw something in them, some deep knowledge and wisdom that he could not put into words. Her eyes spoke of his father's and his own need to communicate beyond the tangible and the everyday.

They made an agreement—primarily driven by Elsie—not to rush into marriage. Elsie considered herself "modern" in the sense that she did not need a man to complete her identity, echoing her mother's belief that a woman's first duty was to herself. She saw her primary mission to assist, not to take care of, her father and sisters in the restful atmosphere of Glen Eyrie. Will Palmer would not have stood in her way if at any time in her relationship with Leo Myers she voiced a desire to marry. But presently, her life was a happy one, filled with concern for her friends and her bountiful life in the Rockies.

On September 6, 1901, Leo's twentieth birthday, an assassin fired two shots at President William McKinley, shattering the stability and optimism of the new century. McKinley died several days later. On September 14, Theodore Roosevelt took the oath as the twenty-sixth President of the United States. For General Palmer it meant that a leader with serious interests in Colorado and western issues was in the White House.

But on another level, the murder of William McKinley, the third presidential assassination in thirty-one years, was sad and worrisome. Will was sorrowful for the country having to endure yet another act of violence directed at the nation's leader.

The assassination was troubling enough for Alice and Joseph Carr in England to reconsider sending their daughter, Dorothy Comyns Carr, to America to visit the Palmers at Glen Eyrie. Other reports of killings and muggings in New York vexed them further. Dorothy Carr was a good friend of the Palmer daughters, particular Dorothy "Dos" Palmer. Both Dorothys were in their early twenties. An adventurous, footloose young woman, Dorothy Carr was eager to see America and General Palmer's version of the Old West, a region made famous around the world by tales of cowboys, warring Indians, and fast guns. She left Southampton, England, in December 1902, bound for America.

Dorothy Carr's diary describing her nine-month sojourn with the Palmers provides insightful glimpses of Glen Eyrie from an outsider's point of view. Like so many pilgrims before her, she was repulsed by the dreariness of the prairies and their "instant" towns appearing like "they had been thrown down on the plain."[4] Arriving at Glen Eyrie in a snowstorm, she declared it "looked like the end of the world—it cannot be the same world that holds England."[5]

This alien land may have at first frightened her but she was undeterred. In the spirit of Rose Kingsley several decades before,

Palmer with friends camping in an aspen forest near Queen's Canyon. The camera shy lady on the far right is Dorothy Palmer. Courtesy of the Starsmore Center for Local History, Colorado Springs Pioneers Museum.

she donned her hiking boots, temporarily packed away her British propriety, and headed out on several walking forays with General Palmer, Elsie, Dos, and sometimes Marjory. Queen's Canyon and Garden of the Gods became Dorothy's favorite locales, filled as they were with "tier on tier of red rock almost joining overhead where the eagle nests are ..." At first she felt "the tenderfoot on western things and customs," but soon she gained stamina and hurried ahead of the Palmers.[6]

On cold winter nights they lounged around the fire at Glen Eyrie. One particular evening they sat taking turns reading thrilling Civil War stories, until it came to Dorothy Carr, who burst into tears upon relating a grisly battle tale.

Carr also commented on an incident at Glen Eyrie. When word of General Palmer's philanthropy was made public, uninvited guests

Palmer with family members and friends in upper Queen's Canyon, circa 1904. Dorothy sits to his right; Peter Harrison stands to his left. Courtesy of the Starsmore Center for Local History, Colorado Springs Pioneers Museum.

showed up at Glen Eyrie hoping to line their wallets with some evidence of his goodwill. On one occasion two nuns arrived at the house asking for a dose of charity. They cited that the general's wealth might preclude him from entering heaven, and therefore it would behoove him to help fund an orphanage in Colorado Springs. Will consented, not because of the threat of eternal damnation, but because the town needed such a place.

In May 1903, President Roosevelt made a whistle-stop in Colorado Springs bringing his message of the proposed Panama Canal and what it could do for the United States and the West. The dutiful Palmers attended the rally in front of the Antlers Hotel, but the visiting Briton was not impressed, claiming that the President made "a mediocre speech—very military in tone—and looked fat and ordinary and rather coarse."[7]

The Palmers took Dorothy to all the tourist spots on her whirlwind wind trip around Pikes Peak and its environs. In Cripple Creek, after dropping down a mine shaft and watching the workers tunneling through a gold vein, Carr proclaimed the experience "unique," but thought the area a "hideous" place. Her English experiences had not prepared her for the mountains of garish mine tailings that covered the hillsides. That summer she roamed around Queen's Canyon, "killed five rattlesnakes," fell ill, and by autumn was ready for the voyage back to England.[8]

Dorothy Carr's trip was just part of the two-way traffic between Colorado Springs and Great Britain. Over the next few years, Alma and Peter Harrison were regular guests of the Palmers. Will's daughters returned often to see their English friends and acquaintances. It was the beginning of a golden era in trans-Atlantic travel, culminating in the loss of the *Titanic* in 1912, when steamship companies built larger and more efficient ships to accommodate both travelers and immigrants.

Hoping to follow in the footsteps of John Singer Sargent, thirty-five-year-old Lawrence Alexander "Peter" Harrison was creating a promising career as a landscape artist. He continued to ride the Impressionist wave that surged across Europe in the late nineteenth and early twentieth century, but he began to cultivate more daring brushwork and bolder colors in his work. He studied in Paris with Artus Van Briggle, who came to Colorado Springs to recover from tuberculosis and opened his pottery studio there in 1901. Peter, Alma, and his brother Leonard "Ginx" Harrison, traveled with Sargent and artist Alfred Parsons on trips to the Continent as well as some of the more provincial hamlets along the Avon and Thames Rivers. In 1902, Peter Harrison was painted by the Italian-French portrait artist Giovanni Boldini, who captured Harrison's angular features and his suave, decidedly vain, manner.

At about this time, Peter began a relationship with Dorothy Palmer, who was nearly twenty-two years old. At first playful and flirtatious, their relationship developed over the years into a romantic one. Even though Peter was happily married to Alma, Dos Palmer and he openly traveled together and often made public their coupleship. "Dos is the most lovely thing I have beheld in many ways," he wrote in a letter, "and sometimes I feel I have not cared enough."[9] Harrison had another girlfriend, Polly Barnard, who was also a member of Sargent's entourage. Sargent painted several watercolors and oil sketches of Dos and Peter in relaxing poses while resting in the summer shade of an alpine forest. During the summer of 1905, for example, Sargent and his party were in the Italian Alps. The group included Peter, Ginx, Alma, Dos, and Polly Barnard. Sargent painted the group as they rested in the flickering shade of a tree, their poses suggestive of closeness and familiarity to each other. Sargent liked, pictorially speaking, the tall lean figures of Dos and Peter, and he staged the scene to take advantage of these artistic features. Dorothy Palmer confirmed her part in the painting in a 1949 letter to art historian David McKibbin: "It was at Breuil in the Italian Alps with the Harrisons and Mr. Sargent and Polly Barnard—he sketched us all there."[10] Other sketches of Dos and Peter followed; one was scheduled for exhibition at Britain's Royal Academy in London, but for some reason that did not materialize. Although Sargent did not feature Dos in a full-length portrait, as he had with her sister, Elsie, he clearly admired her figure. And throughout his friendship with Dos and Peter, he never passed judgment on their relationship.

Peter Harrison also confided in Elsie Palmer, writing her eight- to ten-page letters two to three times a week between 1902 and 1904. Lacking good social boundaries, Peter often resorted to swooning tales of his love for her. Elsie did not discourage him, despite his confessions being highly dramatic and crossing the line between friendship and romantic love. She was in love with Leo Myers at the same time. It was apparent through her letters that such a relationship with Peter caused her deep stress and vexation; but she could not let it go. Harrison told her in one letter: "I thought long of you and how deep the bond is between us—how you keep one alive with a blessed discontent."[11] In another letter he confessed: "Darling Elsie, there is no one like you. You are the only one who can walk straight in and sit down in my palace."[12] He closed one missive with: "Goodnight dearest—sleepwalk and I am *there*."[13]

The general liked Alma and Peter and enjoyed their company when they visited Glen Eyrie. What he privately thought of the relationship between his daughter and Peter is not known, but he probably would have warned her that only heartbreak could come from the futile pursuit of a married man. In Colorado Springs, Peter joined a legion of other admirers of the scenery near Pikes Peak and Garden of the Gods. In 1906, he painted a lively impressionistic view of the estate with Dos and Marjory sitting in the grass in front of the castle. He took advantage of the spring weather, concentrating on the apple green blooms and pale umber tones of April. The area also attracted painters of note, such as Thomas Moran, famous for his views of Yosemite and Yellowstone, who stopped at the glen, conversed with General Palmer, and set up his easel near the Gateway Rocks.

Palmer stands amid some happy campers, circa 1905. A smiling Elsie stands to his right. Courtesy of the Starsmore Center for Local History, Colorado Springs Pioneers Museum.

In early 1903, Will began implementing his ambitious plan to enlarge and renovate Glen Eyrie. In an age of architectural one up-manship, he entertained no thoughts of trying to compete with the Vanderbilts, Carnegies, Pullmans, or the Winchesters. With several modifications here and there, his plan had not changed since he and Queen had begun dreaming of it several years before: a functional, impressive, comfortable English Tudor-style house along the lines of several British country homes he had seen over the years. Although the English Gothic Revival style had witnessed some decline recently, he wanted no other because no other fit so nicely with his and Queen's idea of a home.

An additional consideration for the grand house may have been his daughters' future plans. He had become used to his loneliness, and in some cases, enjoyed the insularity that his estate provided from the city. He did, however, welcome the nearness of his daughters and their friends. Was he in some way making the house as "English" as possible to keep his daughters from fleeing back to Europe? He knew that he could not keep them near him forever, but perhaps the additional lure of a house modeled on a Sussex estate might prolong their sojourn in Colorado.

He commissioned the forty-one-year-old architect, Frederick Sterner, for the job of transforming Glen Eyrie into the house we recognize today. Palmer hoped that the designer of the second Antlers Hotel would bring the same stylish looks to his residence. Sterner was familiar with most architectural eras—Georgian, Queen Anne, Palladian, Classical, and Baroque—but he favored the Gothic tradition, especially for large country houses.[14]

Around the glen the countryside was changing. Homes were encroaching on the mesa as the town stretched westward and north. Even the Garden of the Gods faced the folly of man's desire to improve on nature. In 1903, local businessman Robert McReynold proposed that the Garden be turned into an even greater tourist lure by suggesting that the faces of the three assassinated presidents—Lincoln, Garfield, and McKinley—be carved on the Gateway Rocks.

Palmer was furious, but calmly said that, "such a mutilation of natural scenes would not be in the best taste."[15]

Palmer wanted a blend of innovation and tradition in his new mansion. Outside, however, he preferred as little ostentation as possible. He would have telephones, electricity, and modern plumbing. He, Sterner, and Palmer's engineer, Edmund van Diest, planned a spectacular book hall with soaring beam ceilings and space to accommodate three hundred people. Traditional Gothic features such as lancet windows, carved wood screens, and leaded glass would be used in the mainly masculine downstairs rooms. Wood—carved, smoothed, decorated, and polished—filled the library and staircases. The new structure would be built around the original building; once the building was complete, the inside form would be removed, leaving a sixty-five room, luxurious castle complete with living room, dining hall, kitchen, butler's pantry, Turkish baths, and a special room designed for an ice-making machine. Atop the house a large bell, cast by Krupp of Essen, Germany, would be installed on the roof garden. Used for special events, the bell could be heard for a distance of six miles.[16] The pinkish red granite was quarried in nearby Bear Creek Canyon, which produced a façade of unusual lightness and grace.

Although architectural purists would have scoffed at the thought of an English Gothic house square in the foothills of the American Rockies, Palmer was thrilled with the plan and the implementation. He reasoned that if he loved it, the town would love it also. When it was competed in 1904, the city turned out in horse buggies and horseless carriages to witness their new castle only a stone's throw and a few hills or so from the sin dens of Colorado City. Most agreed it was a suitable addition to "Little London," even though it was a grand house in the country.

At the same time, across town at Colorado College, plans were underway for a large science building to honor the legacy of General Palmer. Like cities, colleges develop over decades, even centuries, and therefore they reflect a patchwork of architectural styles. Colorado College is no exception. At the turn of the century, protégés of Boston architect Henry Hobson Richardson, who died in 1886, were still promoting what would later be called "Richardsonian Romanesque," a building style that in its original form predated English Gothic. A medieval design, it featured semicircular roman arches, heavy, rusticated walls, and picturesque, tiled rooflines.

Colorado College President William Slocum, who hailed from Massachusetts, sought Richardson's style for his new $250,000 Palmer Hall, a style not much appreciated by the general since he was building his domain in Tudor Gothic. The only feature that could please Palmer was to substitute English green tile for the proposed Spanish red tile, and once this material change was agreed upon, the building could proceed.[17] Constructed of Manitou red sandstone, Palmer Hall joined its Gothic and Romanesque neighbors, and as the years passed more modern designs were added to the mix.

The actual construction of Glen Eyrie took place in mid-1903 and into the following year. The Palmers planned a long vacation in Europe while the work was being accomplished.

When the Palmers left for Europe they were fashionably dressed: Will wore his best tweeds and the girls donned long flowing skirts, their hair swept upward in the style of the Gibson Girl. They sailed in one of the new ocean liners capable of carrying three thousand people across the Atlantic. Will once again enjoyed the breezy tonic of a sea voyage, his "lean tireless figure pacing the deck," or ambling up the ladders to get the best view of the rolling and tossing mountains of water.[18] After arrival, Elsie, Dos, and Marjory became accustomed "to the sudden changes of plan that would sweep the whole great party at a few hours' notice from the sunshine of Italy to the snows of winter in Berlin; the tireless sightseeing that exhausted his companions relay by relay ... France, Italy, Greece."[19] Along the way, whether by the cobalt sea near Amalfi or in a pleasant café off the main street in Chartres, they shopped for items and furnishings for their new home in Glen Eyrie.

In London, Will posed for a three-quarter length portrait by Hubert von Herkomer. One of the most versatile painters of Queen Victoria's and Edward VII's court, the Bavarian-born Herkomer was a distinguished Royal Academician and celebrated portrait artist. Like native and non-native British artists, he had risen through the ranks of illustrators and genre painters to become one the most sought-after artists of the day. For nine years he was Slade Professor of Fine Art at Oxford, a position initiated and held by John Ruskin. Although today not as well recognized or honored as John Singer Sargent, he easily moved in Sargent's company at the turn of the twentieth century. For Palmer, it was a privilege to sit in Herkomer's studio during the process.

Will was thrilled by the finished product, a stately aristocratic portrait showing the laird of Glen Eyrie striking the pose of an English country squire. He is dressed in riding breeches and carries a crop, his easy yet dignified manner suggesting he is just about to leave for a ride. Although not as iconic as Sargent's portrait of Elsie, it is nonetheless an artful depiction of the founder of Colorado Springs. After arriving in America, it was hung in a central place in the newly dedicated Palmer Hall at Colorado College.

After leaving the froth and sophistication of Edwardian London, the group headed to the Frant area of Sussex, home to the Mellens. Three of Queen's half-sisters were married and lived near the village, as did Mrs. Ellen Clarke Mellen. Most of the Mellen family remained in England through the early decades of the twentieth century, except Charlotte "Lottie" Mellen, who later played a significant role in the Glen Eyrie legacy and was often referred to as Palmer's "fourth daughter" because of her closeness to the general.

Will Palmer had helped financially support the Mellens through their various life experiences. After divorcing her first husband and with the general's assistance, Lottie took her two sons to England in 1892 and enrolled them at Eton, one of Britain's premier public schools. While there she met and fell in love with the science master, William Lutley Sclater, a noted ornithologist.

They were married in February 1896, and when William was appointed curator of the South African Museum, they sailed for Cape Town. It was the worst of all possible times to make a move to South Africa, as the country was soon embroiled in what developed into the Boer War, one of Britain's fatal imperialistic efforts to hold onto a strategic colony. In one of the first major conflicts of the twentieth century, the British squared off with the Boers, who were the descendants of seventeenth-century French and Dutch settlers in the Transvaal region of South Africa.

Lottie and William found themselves in harm's way. The city was turned into a military outpost, as battalions of khaki-garbed British tommies leading horses draped in guns trooped by their house near the Mount Nelson Hotel. On their way to the Front, north of Cape Town, the soldiers streamed in from the ports and threaded their way through the streets, winding in laden caravans up the hills and into the countryside beyond.

Journalists soon descended on Cape Town to cover the war, including Richard Harding Davis, Winston Churchill, and Rudyard Kipling. Pacing up and down the lobby of the Mount Nelson Hotel, they chafed for action, often getting in each other's way, swapping war stories from previous conflicts, and urging military commanders to let them accompany the troops to the Front. "Cape Town is a dusty wind-ridden western town," noted Davis, "with a mountain back of it that one man said was a badly painted backdrop." The mountain and the hotel, thought Davis, were the only desirable parts of the city.[20]

Meanwhile, Lottie and William hunkered down in their home. While William was busy with his curating duties at the museum, Lottie helped with relief efforts at the local hospital assisting wounded soldiers back from the Front. After the war, Lottie was awarded the Royal Red Cross by Edward VII for distinguished work as a military nurse during the Boer conflict. William continued his scientific work, completing the *Fauna and Flora of South Africa* while stationed in Cape Town.

During and after the war, Lottie kept in close contact with General Palmer and his daughters, visiting Glen Eyrie on several occasions. In 1905, her husband, now forty-two years of age, resigned from the museum in Cape Town following a disagreement with the trustees. Palmer offered the Sclaters a place to live at Glen Eyrie and William a professorship at Colorado College.

By the time the Sclaters sailed for America and a new life in Colorado Springs, the Palmers were back from their European buying trip and settling into their new mansion at Glen Eyrie.

At first it was overwhelming, especially for the daughters who drifted from room to room, upstairs and downstairs, giggling and swooning over the new spacious interior. The general roamed, too, proud that his and Queen's conception was finally realized.

The grounds of Glen Eyrie were always works in progress. Architectural drawings had been prepared for such additional buildings as a carriage house, gardener's house, greenhouses, horse shelter, power plant and laundry, rose arbor and summer house, and a lodge and pavilion. Along the north side of the glen, a tourist drive was constructed for interested people to view the landscape and gardens below. Palmer's holdings included nearly four thousand acres and stretched to the south, along Camp Creek, and over the adjoining mountain. Tourists were generally always welcome, except those who threatened the natural habitats of eagles and hawks.

Occasionally a few famous people motored or rode in, such as the time the general and his daughters entertained the novelist, poet, and mid-western raconteur, Hamlin Garland. The writer was rambling with his wife, Zulime, in the West and was eager to pay the general and the estate a visit. In his Pulitzer Prize–winning biography, *ne* (1922), he described a lavish lawn party on the grounds of Glen Eyrie hosted by the Palmers:

> That journey across the mesa was like a journey into some foreign country—passage to a land which was neither America or England, neither East nor West ... We entered through a most beautiful garden in which all the native shrubs and wildflowers had been assembled and planted with exquisite art. People were streaming in over the mountain roads, some on horseback, some on bicycles, some in glittering, gaily painted wagons, and when we reached the lawn before the great stone mansion, we found a very curious and interesting throng of guests and in the midst of them, the general, tall soldierly, clothed in immaculate linen and wearing a broad western hat, was receiving his friends assisted by his three pretty young daughters. The house was a veritable chateau; the garden was a wonderland of Colorado plants and flowers, skillfully displayed along the bases of the cliffs ... grounds so beautiful

by reason of nature's adjustment, as well as by the way of the landscape gardener's art that they made the senses ache with a knowledge of the exquisite impermanency. It was a kind of poem expressed in green and gold and scarlet.

As I mingled with the joyous folk, I lost myself. I became an actor in the prodigious and picturesque American social comedy. For stage, we had lawn, banks of flowers, and the massive towers of the castle. For background rose the rugged hills ... It threw my life into commonplace drab. And yet it was factitious. It had the transient quality of a dream in which we were but masqueraders.[21]

Many visitors shared Garland's sense of the surreal when confronted by Glen Eyrie, for Palmer's new estate was difficult for eastern and midwestern folk to comprehend in one or two visits: a stately, fashionable Camelot amid the crags of the Rockies. But only he and Queen knew the difficult and winding road it took to get there.

My Kingdom for a Horse

Lottie and William Sclater arrived at Glen Eyrie in July of 1906. William was to begin teaching that fall at Colorado College and start preparing an ornithological exhibit. They occupied one of the upstairs rooms that overlooked the southern crags and foothills. After they settled in, William began extensive birding expeditions around the Garden of the Gods and Queen's Canyon gathering data on some of the ninety species of birds that inhabited the area.[1] Six years later, his intensive studies would yield the seminal work, *A History of the Birds of Colorado* in two volumes.

The general soon discussed with the Sclaters the possibility of building a home for them on the southern section of his property, near the Gateway Rocks of the Garden of the Gods. Palmer commissioned Colorado architect Thomas Macleren to design and build a seven thousand square foot, two-story house in the Cape Dutch style, similar to the one the Sclaters occupied in South Africa. The house would be ready for the Sclaters to move in the following year, and until such time they rented a house on Wood Avenue in the city.

That summer there were the usual activities on the lawn and into the stretches of the canyon, where Will liked to take picnics with his family and friends. Baskets bursting with fruit and loaves of bread were plunked down in front of the assembled groups, the women dressed in their summer white and pink dresses and flowered hats, the men nattily garbed in ties, vests, and linen jackets, their wide-brimmed hats tipped rakishly over one eye as they mugged for the camera. Everyone left their serious faces at the castle as they enjoyed each other's company in the breathless summer air. Elsie, now engaged to Leo Myers, showed him around the castle and extensive grounds. Alma and Peter Harrison were at Glen Eyrie helping to celebrate the general's seventieth birthday that September.

Horses were ubiquitous at Glen Eyrie. The daughters were good riders, but Lottie excelled at horsemanship. She loved the outdoors more than the Palmer daughters and she often accompanied Will on one of his horseback jogs through the canyon and the Garden of the Gods. Once or sometimes twice a day, Palmer had his horse trainer, Jesse Bass, prepare one of his stallions for a ride. The path over the mesa and into the city was also one of his favorite trails, for it gave him a chance to look east over Colorado Springs and the rolling prairie beyond and muse how much his tidy little temperance resort had blossomed into a bustling metropolis of nearly 25,000 people.

His riding style had not changed over the years, and in fact, it had become more reckless. Whether it was reaching his seventieth year or the growing sense of his own invincibility in life, he pursued his pastime vigorously and intently. Besides, he had come through so many scrapes and survived with only a few bruises and sore bones: Antietam, Murfreesboro, Red Hill, and the Apaches of Arizona to name a few. He had endured a few spills because he knew how to fall and not hurt himself. According to Palmer, he had come through "a least a hundred falls" from a horse in his lifetime.[2] Jesse Bass frequently warned him "not to ride loose-legged, but to grip the horse tightly with your knees," and not to stand in the stirrups trying to point out scenery to his guests.[3]

It was sincere advice that went unheeded.

Late October weather near the eastern foothills of the Rockies can vary from highs of sixty degrees Fahrenheit to lows of a record seventeen degrees above zero. October 27, 1906, dawned clear and chilly and by nine o'clock the temperatures were warming into the forties. It was a perfect day for a ride. The sun rose in a low arc across a cobalt sky, the golden aspen and cottonwoods rustled along the trails in the glen and Garden of the Gods, and the air was crisp and motionless with the previous night's dew still in it.

The general rose early, breakfasted, and asked Jesse to prepare three horses—one for himself, the others for Dos and Marjory, for a ride in the Garden. For some unknown reason, Jesse chose, not one of Will's favorite stallions, but a plug named Schoolboy. Marjory was in an especially buoyant mood, having just become engaged to Captain Richard Wellesley of the British Army. After a morning ride through the Garden, the trio was riding home, heading east, through the Gateway Rocks. From that point on, various eyewitness accounts disagree as to the location of Will Palmer's accident and the force of the spill. Somewhere between the Gateway Rocks and the entrance road to Glen Eyrie, the general's horse stumbled and threw him forward, so that he landed on his head, shoulder, or back. The impact rendered him dazed, helpless, and unable to move his lower limbs. Marjory and Dos dashed for help. A motorist, William Otis, happened to be passing by and rushed over to render assistance to the fallen rider. With Palmer's arm draped over his shoulder, Otis gingerly assisted him across a field, lifted him into the car, and sped to Glen Eyrie to get medical help.

Within an hour of the accident, Dr. Will Swan swung his car into the estate and immediately began assessing the extent of the injury. Palmer lay straddled on a couch downstairs, his staff unwilling to move him to more comfortable surroundings upstairs. Swan's initial notes declared his "patient was pale, pupils widely dilated, anxious expression, extremities cold, entirely conscious, complaining of tingling in all extremities, pulse imperceptible at the wrist, complete loss of voluntary motion, except of the head, which motion was painful."[4]

Dr. Swan was a tuberculosis specialist, so he brought in two other doctors to help identify the extent of the general's injury. The doctors soon explained the injury was an "immediate and complete motor and sensory paralysis below the neck without loss of consciousness," and that the injury lay in the mid-cervical area of the spine around the region of the third, fourth, and fifth vertebrae. Will could move his head and neck and bend his elbows slightly. Other than some slight motor movements, he was paralyzed from the waist down.

A great and palpable gloom fell on the house. All the gaiety and energy that used to burst through the doors and out onto the lawn seemed to vanish in the hours following Palmer's accident. People talked in whispers and muffled voices as nurses and doctors swirled around the stricken patient, who was soon moved to a waterbed to ease the problem of bed sores. The morning papers the following day tried to cover the accident in as much detail as they could garner from first-hand reports. Elsie also did her best to feed reporters information on the incident. The Denver Post later ran its headline: "His Limbs Are Paralyzed," adding that "the grave injury is to his spine, which is said to have been so badly wrenched as to cause partial paralysis of the lower limbs."[5] Two specialists were brought in from Denver to make a prognosis. After surgical intervention was ruled out because of the danger, the doctors confirmed that Palmer would have to live the rest of his life as a quadriplegic.

Throughout November and into early December, dark clouds gathered over the Rampart Range and Pikes Peak, bringing a sense of profound loss and despair, and settling on the general's heart like soft wet snow. The bitter irony was plain to most everyone, including Will: how could a man who rode some of the most rugged trails of the West fall from a horse on a smooth trail half a mile from home? "After a life in the saddle," Palmer admitted to Hamlin Garland, "and while riding across an oat field, my horse stumbles and I am pitched to the ground, and here I lie!"[6] The doctors ordered a wheelchair for him so that he could be mobile around the house. One of his daughters or Lottie pushed him to the window where he could watch the jays and magpies flicker through the trees. Whole days were passed looking at the glen outside, his alienated self calculating how much remaining life there was to kill. His tireless body had always soldiered on no matter the situation, but now it was up to his mind to restore what life he had remaining. Lottie or Elsie would read newspapers and letters to him. He dictated notes to well wishers to one of his aides or nurses. Inexorably, he sunk into the mire of misery.

Doctor Henry C. Watt was brought in to be the general's resident physician. Dr. Watt, an Englishman in his mid-thirties who had arrived in Colorado Springs barely two years before, monitored Palmer hourly. Will liked him from the start; his calm and decisive manner, plus his crisp accent, reassured the general. His daughters liked him, too, especially Marjory, who was planning her wedding to Captain Wellesley.

All lives in the big house were impacted by Palmer's injury. Elsie and Dos had always been footloose sorts, but now they found their travels restricted by their father's condition. Elsie was much in love with Leo Myers, but delayed talk of marriage until they knew how things with her father would proceed. At thirty-four, she knew she was closing in on her remaining child-bearing years, so she was not willing to delay her wedding day too long. Dos had arranged for Peter Harrison to accompany her to England for nursing training. She planned to keep appraised of the general's condition while she was

The General seated in his electric car, circa 1907. Courtesy of the Starsmore Center for Local History, Colorado Springs Pioneers Museum.

gone, and if necessary, hurry back to America.

Around Christmas 1906, Will suddenly broke through his initial despair. He seemed to be sick and tired of being sick and tired. He began dictating Christmas lists for the family and staff. He barked some orders and felt good about being the general again. When Elsie brought to Glen Eyrie the famous Philadelphia neurologist, Dr. Silas Mitchell, Palmer waved the man away. "I'm not insane," he grumbled. The doctor remained for a week anyway, and Palmer ultimately admitted him for a diagnosis, which was no different than the previous ones. Will insisted that Elsie and Marjory proceed with their wedding plans. Elsie worked with the local Episcopal Church to firm up her plans, while Marjory and Captain Wellesley seemed to favor a wedding in England.

In February, Will decided to purchase a new electric car so that he could be driven around the territory and perhaps see some new sights. Electric vehicles were something of a novelty on the streets of Colorado Springs, but as the decade advanced, more and more were spotted on Cascade and Pikes Peak Avenues. Forerunners of the more efficient gasoline-powered cars, the electric cars were nonetheless workhorses of the city dweller. By 1910, the number of registered vehicles for both gas and electric was well over eight hundred.

Palmer had an electric vehicle especially ordered to accommodate his injury, which the *New York Times* reported as "electric surrey, with a reclining chair in place of the customary back seat ... Always fond of open-air exercises, General Palmer has been anxious to obtain an easy riding carriage, in which he would be free from all vibration and jar. An electric vehicle ... especially constructed for ease and convenience has just been ordered. The car will have an extension leather top, and a large reclining chair will be fitted in the rear. The carriage will be shipped in a few days to Colorado Springs."[7] The reported cost for the auto was well over $5,000—the most expensive car on the road in southern Colorado at the time.

When the vehicle arrived at C. G. Strang's garage at short time later, the owner dispatched his teenage mechanic, Glen Martin, to drive it over to the castle so the general could see his new possession. Martin would later become Palmer's resident chauffeur at Glen Eyrie.

Because the vehicle was electric it avoided some of the drawbacks that the general hated about horseless carriages, namely the smell and the noise. Two nurses wheeled Palmer toward the car and a glimmer of hope brightened his eyes. The story of those first few days with the general's shiny conveyance is best told by Martin himself:

> That night, Dr. Watt told me, 'If you jolt him, you'll kill him.' I didn't want any part of such a job but Mr. Strang had told me I'd have to drive, so I did. We put up a charger for the battery. The charge was capable of driving the machine for only twenty or twenty-five miles. We'd go out and the general would always pick the hills and of course the electric couldn't make the distance he wanted to go. We were loaded. Sometimes there'd be two nurses on the side and Dr. Watt. The charge would run out and there we'd be, stopped up in some canyon. We'd have to send someone back to get horses. Finally, Miss Marjory conceived the idea of having a motorcycle follow the car to run back for horses when the charge played out. The general did not like the motorcycle's noise and smell and dust and he made its rider stay a long way off.[8]

After enduring dead batteries and several instances when the car stalled in mud flats awaiting rescue, Palmer decided to buy a large flashy Stanley Steamer with tires the size of wagon wheels and a reputation for going into no-man's land and returning unscathed. "It was a gaudy thing with bright red seats," recalled Martin. "The general thought it would be a fine thing, so he bought it at a terrible price ... It had a flash boiler made with a coil of steel and the firebox was as big as the coach top and you sat on top of the whole thing. It ran on seven hundred and fifty pounds of steam. In addition the coil was heated red hot. The water in the condenser was practically steam and heated the coil. But it could not blow up. At least it never did."[9]

Once Palmer got his taste of car travel, he was unstoppable as a rider in one. His nurses would wheel him down to the car, lift him gently into the specially-prepared seat—"like a spoon seat made of hair and feathers"—throw a blanket over his legs, and Martin would ask him where he wanted to go. "Palmer Park!" ordered the general. Martin knew that the trail to Palmer Park was arduous enough for horses, let alone his Stanley Steamer. Martin tried to negotiate a less difficult route. Will insisted on going to Palmer Park. "Let's go up there to Grand View Point!"—which was at the edge of a cliff in the park. Martin answered that there wasn't a road there yet, only a horse trail.

"Can't this steamer go up that thing?" asked the general.

"Yes, it has the power but it would probably tear the tires to pieces."

"I want to go up there!" barked the general.[10]

Martin took his orders, pointed the steamer in the direction of Palmer Park, and proceeded to head up the pine-studded slopes, shredding two tires on the sharp rocks that clung to the edge of the trail. When they finally got to Grand View Point, Martin braked the car and Will sat for hours drinking in the surrounding landscape. He could see Pikes Peak, the Rampart Range, and the town of Colorado Springs stretching out below. Beyond the mesa in the distance, hidden from view, he could imagine his Glen Eyrie.

When he got back to the estate, he ordered his road engineer, Perley Nichols, to take as many men as he needed and cut a road up to Grand View Point. "Get those teams and men and go out there and make camp tonight."[11]

For several years before his accident, he considered the automobile as man's worst invention. It robbed the air's sweetness after a rain and corrupted the haunting shrill of the redwing blackbird. But now, months after his injury, cocooned in its beast-like carriage, he thrilled to the rush of sensations he experienced while driving over the terrain near his home.

Martin also took him on other excursions, up and around yawning chasms and around hairpin turns.

Elsie worried too much at such times and scolded Martin for taking such dangerous trips. Former Colorado Springs resident, Francis Wolcott, commented on Palmer's adjustment to his injury: "He who had spent his life acquiring rights of way for railways, inveighed against the unlicensed freedom of motors ... But in those terrible years when he faced pain and inaction, his only excitement was to lie prone in a motor driven at breakneck speed."[12]

Nothing stopped the general from his daring outings in the

steamer. Martin recalled:

> The general had never been through the Cave of the Winds and he thought he'd like to see it, although no automobile had ever been driven up there. We took a doctor, two nurses, the valet, and two or three helpers and started up Williams Canyon. At the Narrows there was just enough room to allow a carriage to go through. The top of the car was down and bulged out. I saw both sides were touching and I said, "What will we do?" The general said, "Tear the top off!" and we went right ahead. The bows of the top just stayed there. In his form-fitting case he was lugged through the cave and got stuck in a place called "Fat Man's Misery." The general ordered a saw and had the ledge cut off for his release.[13]

When Palmer's friend, Hamlin Garland, revisited Glen Eyrie in mid-1907, he learned the general was "a helpless cripple." Only a few years before, noted Garland, Will was "riding his horse like a trained cavalry leader ... erect, youthful, with straight thrust of legs and a proud uplift to his head. He had seemed in the prime of life, skilled and confident."[14] But on his return, Garland witnessed a wheelchair-bound man accompanied by Elsie and two wolfhounds. The general was quick to tell Garland that he was not entirely without movement. He could move his left hand and turn his head slightly. As Garland stood speechless, the general ordered Glen Martin to bring the Steamer around so that he could give the novelist an auto tour of the area. Martin drove the general and Garland out the winding road leading to the gate at Glen Eyrie, and then turned south along the east face of the Garden of the Gods. As the vehicle gained speed over the rutted trail, Garland looked at his friend in the seat next to him and recalled, "The crippled man's head bobbing like a ball on a string ... Whatever the pain of the passage had been he refused to display any sign of it. He possessed an unconquerable soul. ... At the end of the ride he was able to return to his wheeled couch and have tea with me."[15]

Snow, sleet, rain, or wind did not deter him. "We shall ride!" he bellowed, as if he was leading a charge at a line of Confederate infantry.

Martin stammered, "But, General, it's impossible." Realizing the snow was three feet deep in the driveway, Martin tried to reason with him. Soon, workers started shoveling the drifts out of the roadway. "Plows were put to work, and in a short time they were making a circuit of the Glen," Martin recalled. "After returning to the castle he was in excellent spirits."[16]

Tales of Palmer's reckless behavior in the Steamer filled the halls of Glen Eyrie and made his daughters shudder, although they would have privately admitted that the general was never happier since his accident. He loved the mountains more than ever. It would have been difficult, nearly impossible, for Will to leave such a place, even as Queen had urged him: the wildness and serenity of the sawtooth Rockies was deep in his bones.

About the time that the Sclaters moved into their new home, christened Orchard House, the general received word that his old unit, the Fifteenth Pennsylvania Cavalry, was scheduled to hold their thirty-fifth reunion in Philadelphia in August 1907. Dr. Watt, now the lead doctor at Glen Eyrie, dampened the general's mood by ordering him to remain home, as such a railroad trip was too dangerous. A disgruntled Will took matters into his own hands. Rather than traveling to Philadelphia he would hold the reunion in Colorado Springs—at his own expense.

In mid-August trainloads of veterans, ranging in age from fifty-eight to eighty-two, stepped off the Pullman cars in Colorado Springs, and for the next nine days were hosted by the general and his staff. In all, two hundred and eighty Civil War soldiers were billeted at the Antlers Hotel and Colorado College and took part in the festivities around town. The events cost Palmer over one million dollars in today's money, but the excitement and pleasure it brought him was incalculable.

On August 20, General Palmer in his Stanley Steamer led the parade in the streets of Colorado Springs "through solid phalanxes of cheering spectators," reported the *Gazette*. Behind the general and the Steamer came the troops of the Pennsylvania cavalry, some marching, some on horseback, with banners fluttering as they made their way down Pikes Peak Avenue and headed toward Platte Avenue. The general was dressed in a spotless white suit, nodding here and there to the festive crowds lining the street. Toward afternoon it rained, one of those vicious downpours for which Pikes Peak is known. The general dismissed his unit and ordered them into hot baths in the Antlers Hotel. "Never before in the history of Colorado," the *Gazette* noted, "has there been such a demonstration of popular sentiment, amounting almost to worship, as was exhibited by the thousands of spectators who packed the streets to honor the first citizen of Colorado and his brave old heroes of the Civil War."[17]

At a later evening at Glen Elyrie, the regiment swelled Book Hall to its capacity as everyone dined and toasted the night away. The teetotaling Palmer opened his liquor room to his guests, and even Glen Martin got swept up in the revelry and stumbled off to bed around midnight. At two a.m. he was awakened by Dr. Watt so that he could drive some inebriated veterans to the Antlers Hotel. The still-tipsy driver did his best to get them back to town without causing injury or death to anyone.[18]

On August 25, after two days of sightseeing, the regiment lined up on the lawn at Glen Eyrie, with Palmer and family in the middle, for a photograph to commemorate the reunion. Yorick, the family Great Dane, sat proudly in front of Will and his daughters. In the background a sloping hill fringed in scrub oak and punctuated with towering rock formations framed the group. The entire week taxed the already frail Palmer, but he would not have had it otherwise.

Will and family were able to have a brief respite before the next major event occurred at Glen Eyrie, the much-anticipated wedding of Elsie and Leo Myers, which took place on January 20, 1908. After a honeymoon in Italy the couple returned to England to their new house near the Myers family home in Cambridge. It was Leo's decision to live in England. He never did care much for the American West and he had chosen Britain so that he could best pursue his ambitions as a writer. Elsie agreed, particularly because it seemed that Leo was on a course that would bring them a settled and happy family life.

Leo and Elsie were excited by the prospect of Leo's literary debut, which was a dramatic poem titled *Arvat*. It was a form that had gained great popularity in the times of Shakespeare, Shelley, and Browning. Published under the name Leopold Hamilton Myers, *Arvat* was written in the form popular with the waning years of the aesthetic movement, although it was a genre being quickly eclipsed by more realistic forms in literature. *Arvat* is rich and opulent, very much in the tradition of Swinburne and Rosetti, and it gave Leo confidence that he could make a go of it as a writer.

Leo continued to hold his father's legacy in high regard. For many years he had been working on an abridged version of his father's thirteen hundred-page work, *Human Personality and its Survival of Bodily Death*, a book that was to have far-reaching influence in the twentieth century. At twenty-six years of age at the time of his marriage to Elsie, he was in need of an occupation. His father had left him a substantial fortune from which he could choose any path he desired. In Edwardian England, the educated "idle rich," as they came to be called, had several endeavors in which they could place their time and talent. The military, the law, and government service continued to be attractive, as did university and secondary teaching. If a man or woman liked to risk one's ego, he or she could go into one of the arts, namely the theater, painting, sculpture, or architecture. He had some aspirations as a dramatist, particularly in the vein of J.M. Barrie or W. Somerset Maugham, who had four plays on the London boards in 1908. A novelist, one with the stature of family friend Henry James or fellow Cambridge alum E. M. Forster, was also an alluring possibility. The year before his marriage to Elsie he had committed himself to writing. Exactly what form his writing would take was still a matter of conjecture.

After the positive critical reception of *Arvat*, and with their first child on the way, Leo began to think seriously of a novel during the summer of 1908. His first attempt would carry him through the next ten years, and during that time his themes tended to repeat those of his father's: spiritualism, anti-materialism, the survival of bodily death, and the soul's longing for immortality. Elsie encouraged him in his quest to understand these difficult issues, and both of them would be called upon in less than a year to put their philosophy into practice.

But that summer of 1908 another significant event held their attention, the wedding of Marjory Palmer to Captain Wellesley in England. Glen Eyrie was feverish with excitement with the prospect of Marjory's impending marriage. But there was alarm at the idea of Will traveling by train and ship to attend the wedding, an idea which continued to trouble Dorothy, who had replaced Elsie as the daughter in charge of the general's well-being. Once again, General Palmer insisted on being at an important family event. Dr. Watt surprised everyone by consenting to the journey to England, as long as certain precautions would be taken during the train trip, the voyage, and during their travels around England. Over the past eighteen months, according to Dr. Pershing, one of Palmer's physicians, the general had "become more sleepless and depressed."[19] Dr. Watt may have weighed the trip to England versus the idea of Palmer's slipping into a worse depression if he remained at Glen Eyrie and decided that the former was a better move. Also, Will thought it prudent to consult a spine specialist in Europe. In any event, the Palmer entourage—Will, Dorothy and Marjory, Dr. Watt and another physician, two nurses, two governesses, Lottie and William Sclater, fourteen staff members, a secretary, and a caterer—left on May 31 from Colorado Springs for the trip across the Atlantic. Glen Martin had preceded them to Liverpool where a new Steamer awaited the Palmers to drive around England.

On June 6 they boarded the S.S. *Minneapolis*. In scenes that could have only been ripped from the pages of a romance novel, the following days held a startling development. We must imagine the characters and the setting as the day unfolded. It was mid-way through the voyage and Will lounges in his wheelchair on deck staring at the sun sparkling on the wind-whipped sea. He imagines that his daughter Marjory will be quite happy with her new beau Captain Wellesley, wherever they choose to reside, although it looks quite likely that it will be in England. So as not alarm her father, Marjory gingerly approaches, sits beside him and gently strokes his arm. After a brief discussion of minor things, she hesitates and then breaks the news: she cannot marry Captain Wellesley and she will tell him as soon as they land in England. Stunned, the general grumbles something but listens intently. Marjory tells him that she is in love with Dr. Watt and that they intend to live in Colorado Springs. And the trip to England? We shall make the best of it, Will decides, and follow through with the plans—without the wedding of course.

And so they did. The wedding was called off and the party prepared their alternate plans. Glen Martin was ready with the Steamer and rounded up extra cars and drivers for the trip south through England and later across the Channel to France. Martin found the British roads not as developed as the French ones. While the British had macadamized some of their thoroughfares, most were muddy and torturous by modern standards. French officials got busy the year before improving their roads to set the stage for the Great Race of 1908, in which several drivers from different countries competed. Traveling from New York to Paris, via Alaska, Asia, and southern Europe, the drivers braved thunderstorms, typhoons at sea, desert sun, mountain snows, and rutted quagmires while enduring the 169-day ordeal. The race was front-page news in both the *New York Times* and the *Times* of London and did much to encourage the improvement of roads in both Europe and America.

The Palmer entourage arrived back in London in time for the birth of Elsie's and Leo's first child, Elsie Queen Myers (later known simply as E.Q.), on November 4, 1908. The birth was somewhat dampened by the news that Palmer's European doctors had not viewed his situation as any more favorable than his American physicians a year before. Any hopes of returning to a life of reasonable bodily movement were gone. Resigned to a life of a quadriplegic, he was taken the following day to the American Consulate in London to sign his last will and testament, which was witnessed and signed by the United States Vice Consul General, Richard Westacott, and two other witnesses.

As to be expected, William Palmer designated his daughters to receive the bulk of his estate; the Mellen siblings received $50,000 each, except Maud who would receive $75,000 for the care of her husband and children; Palmer's staff would receive substantial annuities. Across the board, his family, those who knew him, tolerated him, and those in his employ were the recipients of his generous nature.

On the return voyage to New York, more tragedy struck the general. While being carried in a litter from one deck to the next, his head rolled to the right and struck a rail. "He had to go up there," wrote Glen Martin. "They didn't have an elevator, so they had to carry him up the stairway."[20] Although seemingly minor, the injury, combined with a case of bronchitis, hastened his decline.

Back at Glen Eyrie he listened to the news as read to him by Dorothy or Lottie. He perked up at the idea of a new Republican administration in the White House. On March 4, the portly William Howard Taft took office, replacing Theodore Roosevelt who had distinguished himself by opening the Panama Canal in 1904 and later by flexing American muscle in sending the Great White Fleet around the world. Taft, who once claimed that, "Politics, when I am in it, makes me sick," vowed to implement the bold progressive movements of his predecessor.[21] Dorothy Palmer was perplexed by all the political intrigues that her father seemed to enjoy. Progressives? Conservatives? How did G.K. Chesterton put it? "The whole modern world has divided itself into progressives and conservatives," he wrote dryly. "The business of progressives is to go on making mistakes. The business of conservatives is to prevent the mistakes from being corrected."[22]

In the latter half of 1908, Will gained enough motor movement in his hand to begin writing his own letters. He could scrawl letters one inch high in pencil with fifteen to twenty words per page. He took pleasure in such a simple act, for it gave him some personal liberty as well as being able to be in direct contact with those he loved.

He went through frightful mood swings, happy one day, gloomy the next. Elsie and Leo had come over from England bringing E.Q., his first granddaughter. Maud Mellen VanOstveen's children cavorted on a makeshift swing in his room. Amused and heartened by everyone's presence, he continued writing letters whose content seemed to get shorter and shorter.

He drifted into dreams of the past. Forty years before, he had begun his courtship of Queen Mellen and passionate letters to each other began pouring from their hearts. Will's letters spoke of his hopes of accompanying her to the inaugural ball of General Grant and later how he thought a little railroad "all one's own" would be a fine addition to his planned temperance resort at the foot of Pikes Peak; and how a dream emerged of an English manor house in which he and Queen could raise their children.

They faced many obstacles in their lives, and he could say, thankfully, they overcame most of the important ones.

"On March 10 [,1909]," noted John Fisher in his biography, "he was well enough to go out for a short drive in the grounds of Glen Eyrie; the next day there was a heavy fall of snow, and he stayed indoors, cheerful and contented. That night he slipped from his sleep into a coma from which he never roused again, and on March 13 he died."[23] Palmer was seventy-two.

One of the last family portraits before General Palmer's death in 1909. Leo Myers sits second from the right in the front row with Elsie's hand on his shoulder. Courtesy of the Starsmore Center for Local History, Colorado Springs Pioneers Museum.

Epilogue
Glen Eyrie and Beyond

For the next week or two, the whole city fell into mourning. Cables and letters streamed in from Denver, Pueblo, and from as far away as Italy and Greece. Dos, Marjory, Elsie, and Leo assisted guests who had traveled in for the funeral, which was scheduled for March 17. Among the mourners were the Bells, the Slocums, and the Sclaters.

On a cloudless but cool late winter day, the hearse bearing the cremated remains of William Jackson Palmer left the train station and threaded its way to Evergreen Cemetery. On each side of the hearse stood throngs of Colorado College students who stood silently as the procession passed.

At the cemetery, pine boughs had been strewn along the path to the gravesite. The Reverend Arthur Taft of St. Stephen's Episcopal Church led the ceremony, and quoted passages from the Bible. Leo Myers and Palmer's close business associate, Colonel D. C. Dodge, lowered the urn containing the ashes into the grave. A simple service followed, then the large group clad in black dispersed and climbed into their various vehicles.

Later, President Slocum delivered a poignant and glowing tribute at Colorado College. At one point in his speech, he declared: "The coming of General Palmer was the turning point in the history of this region. From the day he rode over the site of the city, which is today his proudest monument, practically dates all the prosperity this county has experienced. Seeing, he acted. With his boundless faith in the future of this great, unmeasured West, this energetic, clear-sighted pioneer and prophet, this hero of many battles and builder of railroads and communities, mustered the forces which resulted in the founding of the colony and the subsequent development of the Pikes Peak region."[1] Remaining members of the Fifteenth Pennsylvania Cavalry had voted to place a bronze tablet in Colorado College commemorating Palmer's service to his country. Major McAllister gave the dedication speech and said in part: "General Palmer's conduct as a soldier was marked by a prudent temerity. He believed and always acted on the belief that a vigorous, unhesitating attack was conducive to the safety of his command. Many times his prisoners were surprised and mortified that they had been captured and their forces scattered by a body of men a third of theirs in number ... Despite General Palmer's splendid record as a soldier he was essentially a man of peace. He believed that war was a fragment of savagery inherited from the remote ages."[2]

It seems that few people had anything negative to say about General Palmer—and those who did remained in a silent minority. Such was the legacy of the founder of Colorado Springs and the builder of Glen Eyrie.

In 1910, the remains of Queen Palmer were disinterred from an English graveyard and placed beside those of General Palmer in Evergreen Cemetery. A simple Ute Pass stone serves as the monument to their lives together.

Life at the castle was never really the same in the days and months after Palmer's injury. After the patriarch's death, people tried to resume their lives and occupations, inevitably leaving Glen Eyrie. The staff, including nurses, gardeners, and laborers, etc., went their separate ways. Elsie, Dos, and the Sclaters drifted back to England; Marjory stayed in Colorado Springs. By the summer and autumn of 1909, the great house was a beautiful but empty tomb.

Marjory Palmer married General Palmer's physician, Dr. Henry Watt, on September 24, 1909, and the two resided on Culebra Avenue

Dr. Henry Watt and Marjory Palmer in 1915. Courtesy of the Starsmore Center for Local History, Colorado Springs Pioneers Museum.

in Colorado Springs. Dr. Watt became one of the city's most prominent physicians and Marjory helped finance the Sunnyrest Sanatorium in 1910, where she also worked for a brief time. By the first decade of the twentieth century, the city continued to receive hundreds of tuberculosis patients a year. Sunnyrest was one of a number of sanatoriums serving the area and in the first three years it accommodated nearly eighty patients from around the world. Dr. Watt continued to practice medicine until his untimely death in December 1916. Always in fragile health, Marjory stayed in Colorado Springs until the end of the First World War and then joined her sisters in London. She succumbed to tuberculosis in 1925 at the age of forty-four, the same age as her mother Queen at the time of her death.

Lottie and William Sclater left Colorado Springs in 1909 after William was offered the post of chief ornithologist at the Bird Room of the Museum of Natural History in London. They settled near the museum in Kensington Gardens.

In those years before 1914, when people such as Elsie and Dorothy Palmer and the Sclaters settled or in some cases re-settled in England, the cultural shift from the sparsely inhabited Rockies to the suburbs of London seemed a rather significant tremor in their lives. Great Britain still ruled the largest empire in the history of the world, although in many ways its glory was beginning to fade. Socially, the gentry controlled a major portion of the nation's wealth, while the working class toiled for meager wages. There were constant strikes between 1910 and 1914, some involving the mine workers in Cornwall and Wales. Militarily, Britain embraced an entente with Russia and France, which sought to balance the power of Kaiser Wilhelm's Germany. And perhaps more importantly to most Britons was the threat of revolution in Ireland. But if these events were enough to unsettle the most ardent Anglo-Saxon, they did not shake the optimism that characterized the long Edwardian summer—that period of time just before August 1914, after which the world fell apart.

Most Americans find it difficult to comprehend the impact of the First World War—or what is called The Great War in Britain—and its effect on the lives of those who lived through it, just as it is for Britons to understand the effects of the American Civil War on its people. Quickened by the assassination of the heir to the Austro-Hungarian throne in Sarajevo, the war suddenly stormed into English life. Young men by the droves volunteered for action on the Western Front in France and Belgium; whole villages and towns lost a majority of their male youth; those already in the British Army, such as Eric and Cyril Mellen—Lottie and William Sclater's sons—were thrust as junior officers into the thick of the fighting in Flanders.

Many of the officers who fought on the Western Front graduated from English private schools. There were reasons for this. For one thing, young men who attended schools such as Eton and Rugby were well nourished and therefore met the height requirement of the British Expeditionary Force. It has been estimated that twenty percent of those who died in battle were graduates of private schools, versus thirteen percent of the deaths overall during the war. Junior officers—lieutenants and captains—were particularly susceptible to death in battle, as they were typically the first soldiers "over the top." The war took the lives of 1,157 Eton graduates, including those lives of Lottie's two sons, who were killed in action in France.

Trained as a nurse, Lottie found work in the many London hospitals and in country houses converted into makeshift infirmaries. The wounded from the Front were unloaded from trucks that streamed in from Dover. Belgian refugees, fleeing the advance of German troops, also poured into London. Young and middle-aged women, wives and daughters, were pressed into service as nurses as the war escalated and the unimaginable—the carnage in the trenches—became an everyday reality.

The need to serve in some capacity was so great that ordinary citizens volunteered their time and energy. William Sclater combined his duties at the museum with volunteering for the Soldiers' and Sailors' Families Association, a charities group that assisted servicemen's families in need. After the war, he edited the *Zoological Record* from 1919 to 1937 and served as secretary of the prestigious Royal Geographical Society during the Second World War.

During that conflict, Lottie was killed in a German air raid on London in 1942; William died from his injuries in 1944, after a V-1 rocket destroyed his home and the entire section of Sloane Court in London.

Dorothy and Elsie Palmer spent the years 1910 through the mid-1950s in close proximity to each other. Dorothy, who never married, remained the great traveler of the three daughters. In the years before the Great War, she accompanied Sargent and Peter Harrison on several tours of the Swiss Alps and Italy. She loved taking photographs, which were often comical and sentimental in nature, posing jauntily or good-naturedly before a monument or some resplendent scene in the Lake District of England. She was often seen with Peter Harrison, who maintained a happy relationship with his wife, Alma, at the same time. Alma Strettel Harrison continued her work as a translator and poet. Fifty years of age in 1916, Peter was too old to serve with the British Expeditionary Force (BEF) in the First World War but instead volunteered for rear echelon service with the army. He was stationed in Mons and Ypres in Belgium when the stalemate continued on the Western Front, frequently reporting on the conditions of the war to Dorothy, Elsie, and Leo Myers. Dorothy resumed work

Elsie Myers with Elsie Queen (E.Q.) Myers, 1909. Courtesy of the Starsmore Center for Local History, Colorado Springs Pioneers Museum.

with the less fortunate in the London slums of the East End, working in soup kitchens and serving where needed. For many years she helped support the World Federation, an organization devoted to the unification and understanding of different ethnic groups. It could be truthfully said that Queen Palmer raised her daughters with others in mind.

While Dorothy was the traveler and caregiver, Elsie remained the family matriarch and archivist. Little of any detail escaped her perceptive nature. In her youth she collected flowers and plants, placing their petals and leaves inside her diary. After her second daughter, Eve, was born in 1910, she amassed an album of Palmer and Myers memorabilia. She collected and organized most of the correspondence between Queen and Will Palmer, as well as most of the letters within the Palmer family. She kept detailed logbooks of her family and its activities in those seemingly innocent years before the war. She, Leo, E.Q, and Eve often traveled in England and Scotland with Dorothy and one or two of the Mellen clan, who continued to live in several of the small villages in Sussex.

But Elsie's marriage was not a happy one. Leo and she had always been strong-willed and independent individuals, and their marriage and children, instead of bringing them together, forced them further apart. Moreover, Leo was introspective, and as a writer who needed space, he frequently walled himself off for days working on a project.

As they matured, E.Q and Eve felt the strain of the relationship with a father who was not always there for them. In the years before and during the war they lived in East Grinstead in Sussex, and afterwards in Marlow on the Thames River, both locales not far from London.

When the First World War came, Leo worked as a clerk in the Board of Trade. He was thirty-three years old, and when most men of his age were volunteering for service with the BEF, he chose a more pacifist outlet. He was not a coward; many men of his era consciously decided that they could best serve their country by pursuing other, less violent, courses of action. "They also serve who only stand and wait," to quote Milton.

During these difficult years of war and the period thereafter,

Left to right, Leo Myers, E.Q., Elsie, Eve, and Peter Harrison, circa 1916. Courtesy of the Starsmore Center for Local History, Colorado Springs Pioneers Museum.

Leopold Hamilton Myers worked painstakingly on his craft as a writer, becoming better known by his pen name, L.H. Myers. Initials were becoming popular with authors, as they often gave a certain mystique to otherwise commonplace names. They also disguised one's gender, which at times in history proved valuable to certain writers.

The war, however, changed him from a man with a shred of faith in mankind into one who seriously doubted that civilization could continue. The war affected many people in that manner. Leo became part of that generation who staggered out of the carnage of the war and looked beyond Europe for a sustaining faith. Often referred to as the "lost generation," these writers included D.H. Lawrence and T.S. Eliot in Great Britain, and Ernest Hemingway and John Dos Passos in America. Leo studied Eastern religion and mysticism to the degree that his interests replaced his traditional studies in English Literature and Continental Philosophy.

In 1922, after ten years of labor, he published his first novel, *The Orissers*, which met with strong critical acclaim. Its setting was in Britain, not in the Indian subcontinent where most of his attention was now directed. But even though he was to focus the majority of his fiction on India and its religion, he never traveled there.

Elsie and Leo often attended dinner parties of the Bloomsbury group, an informal collection of writers, artists, and intellectuals dedicated to the arts, whose members included Virginia Woolf, Duncan Grant, E.M. Forster, L.P. Hartley, and the sculptor Frank Dobson. Leo always remained on the fringe of this group, no doubt because his strong sense of individualism precluded him from joining any organizations. Even while at Eton and Cambridge, he shunned groups and clubs. In the 1920s, like many disillusioned men and women, he considered joining the Communist party, but later broke with its ideals. In the mid-1920s, he set a course that would cultivate his belief in spiritual transcendence and probe it in his novels.

During this time Elsie and Leo's daughter, E.Q., rose to prominence as a textile designer. In 1931, she married architect Christopher "Kit" Nicholson, with whom she had three children, including the painter Tim Nicholson. E.Q. enjoyed success as a designer throughout her long career; she visited Glen Eyrie and Colorado Springs in 1959.

Leo published his second work of fiction, *Clio*, in 1925, but it was not until the appearance of his novel of India, *The Near and the Far*, in 1929 that he achieved international acclaim. Set in India in the seventeenth century, the novel examines through its set of characters the eternal conflict between the body and the soul and the search for permanence in a world of fleeting sensations. The addition of later novels—*Prince Jali* (1931) and *Rajah Amar* (1935)—form the trilogy published under the title, *The Root and Flower*. It is Myers's most ambitious and mature work, reflecting a life that was both introspective and unhappy.

His characters in *The Root and the Flower*—really projections of himself—search for brief moments of understanding in the complexity of life. At one point in the novel, a distressed male character describes a moment in the garden: "As he stood there amongst the flowers and butterflies the world seemed to him a place of extraordinary beauty. Living appeared to be a wonderfully simple thing after all. You had but to throw away the trouble and worry of taking things unto yourself, and then all the earth would be yours to enjoy in a disinterested ravishment. The striving between man and man would have vanished; Paradise was as simple as that."[3]

Myers thought that only if we could have these brief, reassuring epiphanies life, would be more bearable and happy.

The trilogy has been called a "philosophical" work, an often-dangerous course for any writer because it suggests that his intent is to indoctrinate the reader in the author's views. But this is not the case with Myers's work. His strong characters and vibrant settings only suggest to the reader another way of looking at things. Novels of India were popular after the First World War and in the years before the beginning of World War II; they provided an escape and alternative point of view to the disastrous developments in Europe, as during the period it shifted toward fascism and dictatorship. *The Root and Flower,* called a minor masterpiece by many critics, joined other fine works of India from the same period, notably Forster's *A Passage to India* (1924) and Herman Hesse's *Siddhartha* (1922).

Happy and somber occasions always brought the Palmer sisters together and this happened in 1936 with the death of Peter Harrison at the age of seventy. Both Elsie and Dorothy were saddened by the loss. Peter and the Palmer sisters had shared their deepest joys and sorrows over the years. After a period of grief, Elsie emerged once again. She assisted her father's first biographer, John Fisher, by organizing her collection of correspondence for use in the biography, which appeared in 1939 and helped spread the legend of the founder of Colorado Springs.

Like his characters, Leo Myers searched for spiritual certainty, but when he thought he found it, life was not as sweet as it once was. He grew more isolated and despondent. He quarreled with most of his friends. Some he kept: he had befriended George Orwell with a loan so that the author could travel to North Africa to recover from tuberculosis. The arrival of the Second World War in 1939 seemed like a repeat of the nightmare of the Great War, as England faced yet another threat from Germany. As the war progressed, British and enemy fighters fought over the skies of the Myers's home on the Thames River.

He wanted life to be more spiritual; he wanted people to be more selfless and less materialistic; and when life and people could not meet his expectations he rejected them. He once asked, "Why should anyone want to go on living once they know what the world is like?" On April 7, 1944, at the age of sixty-four, he ended his life by taking an overdose of Veronal, a sleep medication.[4]

After Leo's death, Dorothy helped comfort Elsie, and when the war ended, their lives brightened. They spent summers together reminiscing about their days in Colorado, about their father, the general, and the smell of his riding boots in the closet at Glen Eyrie, and their mother, Queen, who schooled them in the loveliness of natural things.

Elsie died of natural causes in 1955.

Dorothy passed away in 1961.

And now, Glen Eyrie, the other member of the family.

For many years after General Palmer's death and exodus of the family and staff, Glen Eyrie languished in search of proper stewards.

Will and Queen would have felt disheartened in those years as the estate encountered its uncertain fate.

After the daughters tried and failed to sell it to the city of Colorado Springs, the estate fell into disrepair and the gardens left overgrown. Awaiting a buyer, Glen Eyrie entered the years of the First World War, and that point, no one was too willing to take on Glen Eyrie at the hefty price of over $100,000.

In 1916, a group of investors known as the Oklahoma Syndicate purchased Glen Eyrie for $150,000, in hopes of turning it into a country club and resort. They projected that over the next few years, one hundred and fifty villas would be built in and around Queen's Canyon. They began charging admission to Glen Eyrie and by 1918 the group had earned over $45,000. The project's failure came as a welcome relief to most of the city's residents who continued to hold General Palmer's memory in high regard.

By the end of 1917, Glen Eyrie was not the only architectural attraction in the region. Despite the conflict in Europe and stagnating real estate prices, Spencer Penrose, a Philadelphia speculator who made millions in the Cripple Creek gold strike, eyed a resort near Cheyenne Mountain. He at first approached Glen Eyrie architect Frederick Sterner, who was presently working in New York. But after Sterner reneged on the project, Penrose hired the firm of Warren and Wetmore to complete his magnificent edifice in the foothills of the Rockies. The unsettling years of 1917–18 and America's entry into the First World War did not deter Penrose, as he spearheaded the construction of the Broadmoor Hotel. At a cost of well over a million dollars, the Broadmoor exceeded the size, scope, and elegance of anything in the Rockies. He used the design of many European hotels and resorts to arrive at his Italian Renaissance creation, which scheduled its opening for June 1, 1918.

The construction, advertising, and marketing of the Broadmoor resort drew attention away from Glen Eyrie into the decade of the 1920s. In 1918, Glen Eyrie was purchased by Alexander Cochran, a rug manufacturer, yachting enthusiast, and sportsman, who came to Colorado to recover from tuberculosis, which was perhaps his sole reason for buying the estate. He wed the twice married and divorced Polish opera singer, Ganna Walska. The two were rarely seen together at Glen Eyrie and were divorced in 1922. Cochran enlarged the property to 6,580 acres and initiated a program of commercial gardening. Cochran employed the German immigrant, Eugene Burghard, to supervise the extensive grounds and gardens. Cochran died in 1929, leaving Glen Eyrie once again to await a suitable buyer.

Glen Eyrie weathered the Great Depression but it was apparent that it needed more than an indifferent occupant or someone using it as an occasional home. During this period minimal maintenance was carried out on the property. In 1938, Texas oilman George Strake bought the estate and added the Pink House and two swimming pools. But like Cochran, Strake had several homes in other parts of the West and spent only a few months a year in the house. Strake's wealth was estimated between 100 and 200 million dollars, but it is noteworthy that he did not use his money to overdevelop or try to enhance the property in a way inappropriate for its setting.

By the beginning of the Second World War, the taste for Gothic Revival had run its course. It was replaced with more modern styles that emphasized the elimination of excessive decoration and stressed a more "functional" look. As the city of Colorado Springs began a growth spurt after the First World War, it increased its cultural centers at Colorado College and downtown as well. One of the most important of these additions was the Fine Arts Center, which was established in 1936 and funded by philanthropist Alice Bemis Taylor. The architect for the Center was Santa Fe-based John Gaw Meem, who employed a combination of Pueblo and Spanish Colonial styles in the design. Built at the height of the Depression, the center's design was a bold departure from the traditional styles seen around town. In 1966, the Arts Center acquired John Singer Sargent's Miss Elsie Palmer from the Albright-Knox Art Gallery in Buffalo, New York, thereby sending the portrait to the city of Elsie's childhood home. It hangs there today, still fascinating residents and tourists alike.

After years of neglect, Glen Eyrie was purchased in 1953 by the Christian group called the Navigators, who were interested in using it as a headquarters, a training base for missionaries, and a year-round conference center. Currently it stills serves those functions,

Glen Eyrie, present day.

although its role has been expanded more to serve the community. In 1984, the Navigators inaugurated an ecological plan for the canyon, which protected the natural environment, added walking trails, and organized several wildlife watching efforts. Many of General Palmer's attitudes toward preserving and enhancing the natural environment were restored, such as emphasizing conservation and avoiding ostentation and excessive design features.

Today, nearly one and fifty years after workers built Will and Queen's original house, the canyon and Glen Eyrie itself still look remarkably wild and pristine. Even the thousands of trees added during and after General Palmer's lifetime have not tamed the look of Queen's Canyon. Over the years the suburbs of Colorado Springs have crept ever closer to the estate, but thanks to the presence of the intervening mesa and Garden of the Gods to the south, the advance of civilization has been kept at bay.

Although Queen Palmer did not get a chance to experience the luxury of Glen Eyrie's final phase, she was there during the time when Colorado Springs was built literally from the ground up. Her view of Glen Eyrie included days spent in tents and the barn while the original construction was continuing, and later when Ute Indians wandered into the canyon and stared through her windows. General Palmer could look back on those early days with satisfaction as he carved a little niche in the Wild West for his wife and daughters. He had witnessed the founding of a city and watched his modest dream house evolve into a grand castle where he brought his daughters and their suitors. He had spent only five years or so in the new Glen Eyrie but they were charmed and later difficult years full of life's richness and joy.

And now, amid the squawk of blue jay and the tread of deer and elk, the manor house nobly stands—ready for the next one hundred years.

Notes

Except where otherwise noted, all the letters, diaries, and journals cited in the notes are from the original sources archived in the Starsmore Center of the Pioneers Museum of Colorado Springs, Colorado. The museum contains an extensive collection of historical records from the early life in the city. Additional primary sources are also located at Tutt Library, Colorado College, the Navigator Archives, and the Pikes Peak Library District archives, also in Colorado Springs. In 1905, General Palmer's friend, Isaac Clothier, self-published a slim volume of their early letters to each other.

The Horse Soldier

1. John Fisher, A Builder of the West, p. 28.
2. William Jackson Palmer (WJP) to Isaac Clothier, Letters, p. 18.
3. Ibid, p. 123.
4. Ibid, p. 127.
5. Fisher, p. 68.
6. John Palmer to WJP, April 2, 1862. William's parents, John and Matilda Palmer, had three other children. John died in 1863; Matilda later moved to Colorado where she died in July 1898, age 93.
7. Matilda Palmer to WJP, June 10, 1862.
8. WJP to Isaac Clothier, Sept. 6, 1861.
9. WJP to John Palmer, April 23, 1862.

10.   Fisher, p.87.
11.   Ibid, p. 90.
12.   Ibid, p. 89.
13.   Ibid, p. 94.
14.   Ibid, p. 100.
15.   Clothier, p. 36.
16.   William A. Bell, New Tracks in North America, p. 175.
17.   Ibid, p. 195.
18.   Ibid, p. 200.
19.   Fisher, p. 147.
20.   WJP to Queen Palmer, October 28, 1869.
21.   WJP to QP, June 11, 1869.

This Above All

1.   Cecilia Black, Queen of Glen Eyrie, p. 15.
2.   Ibid.
3.   WJP to QP, February 20, 1869.
4.   Ibid, June 11, 1869.
5.   Ibid, April 5, 1869.
6.   Ibid, October 7, 1869.
7.   Ibid, August 7, 1869.
8.   Ibid, January 17, 1870.
9.   Ibid, May 21, 1870.
10.   Ibid, May 15, 1870.
11.   Ibid, January 30, 1870.
12.   Ibid, February 7, 1870.
13.   Marshall Sprague, Newport in the Rockies, p. 14.
14.   WJP to QP, March 9, 1870.
15.   Queen Palmer's journal, November 9, 1870.
16.   QP's journal, November 9, 1870.
17.   Sprague, Newport, p. 12.
18.   Ibid, p. 18.
19.   Tim Blevins, ed., Legends, Labors and Loves, p. 216.
20.   Ibid, p. 215.

Queen of Hearts

1.   WJP to QP, November 2, 1871.
2.   Rose Kingsley, South By West, p. 23.

3. Ibid, p. 24.
4. Rocky Mountain News, November 18, 1871.
5. Kingsley, p. 27.
6. Ibid, p. 30.
7. Marshall Sprague, Newport in the Rockies, p. 28.
8. Kingsley, p. 31.
9. Ibid, p. 32.
10. Ibid, p. 33.
11. Ibid, p. 35.
12. Ibid, p. 36.
13. Cecilia Black, Queen of Glen Eyrie, p. 76.
14. Sprague, p. 78.
15. Black, pp. 76–77.

Tales of Little London

1. Tim Blevins, ed., Legends, Labors and Loves, p. 217.
2. Ibid, p. 218.
3. Ibid, p. 227.
4. Marshall Sprague, Newport in the Rockies, p. 67.
5. Ibid, p. 30.
6. Quoted in Blevins, ed. Labors, p. 30.
7. QP's journal, February 3, 1875.
8. John Fisher, A Builder of the West, p. 285.
9. Ralph Edgar Bailey, Fight for the Royal Gorge, p. 140.
10. Irving Stone, Men to Match My Mountains, p. 440.

English Hours

1. WJP to QP, April 26, 1862.
2. Ibid, January 2, 1882.
3. WJP to Elsie Palmer, December 30, 1882,
4. Marshall Sprague, Newport in the Rockies, p. 88.
5. Elsie Palmer's diary, September 30, 1883.
6. Quoted in Fisher, p. 283.
7. Ibid, p. 284.
8. Elsie Palmer to George Macdonald, undated.
9. Elsie Palmer's diary, no date.
10. Henry James to John Singer Sargent, June 2, 1884.
11. Richard Ormond, Sargent, p. 34.

12. The Mote is the setting for Anya Seton's classic gothic novel, Green Darkness.
13. Henry James to Ruth Norton, September 9, 1887.
14. James wrote 15 letters to Queen between 1887 and 1893.
15. QP to WJP, September 21, 1887.
16. Ibid, October 23, 1887.
17. Ibid, September 20, 1890.
18. Alice Carr, Reminiscences, p. 64.
19. John Fisher, A Builder of the West, p. 291.
20. Henry James to Ruth Norton, January 3, 1889.
21. QP to WJP, perhaps unsent, July 1886.
22. QP's journal, March 8, 1889.
23. Ibid, March 9, 1889.
24. Ibid, March 16, 1889.
25. Ibid, March 21, 1889.. 16.
26. Ibid, March 25, 1889.

Portrait of a Lady

1. Fred Kaplan, Henry James, p. 271.
2. Quoted in Richard Ormond, Sargent,
3. Alexa Hayes, "Confronting Elsie Palmer," p. 60
4. Alice Carr, Reminiscences, p. 123.
5. Ormond, p. 139.
6. The Times, May 8, 1891.
7. Magazine of Art, 1891, pp. 261–262.
8. Ormond, p. 35.
9. Dorothy Palmer's journal, August 7, 1893.

Nomads

1. Quoted in Stephen J. May, Maverick Heart, p. 36.
2. Marshall Sprague, Newport in the Rockies, pp. 98–99.
3. Tim Blevins, ed., Legends, Labors and Loves, p. 224.
4. Sprague, p. 153.
5. Elsie Palmer to QP, December 25, 1894.
6. Elsie Palmer's diary, December 28, 1894.
7. Blevins, ed. p. 278.
8. Manitou Springs Journal, January 30, 1896.

9.   Sprague, p. 159.
10. Arthur Schlesinger, Jr., ed., Almanac of American History, p. 387.
11. Arthur Lubow, The Reporter Who Would Be King, p. 140.
12. Philip Knightley, The First Casualty, p. 55.
13. Schlesinger, ed., p. 63.
14. WJP speech to Mahogany Club, December 8, 1897.
15. Ibid.
16. WJP to Isaac Clothier, Letters, p. 298.
17. Knightley, p. 56.
18. WJP to George Peabody, March 8, 1898.
19. Quoted in Schlesinger, p. 68.
20. WJP to President McKinley, March 30, 1898.
21. H.R. Brands, T.R.:The Last Romantic, p. 337.
22. Blevins, ed., p. 49.
23. Ibid.
24. WJP to Colonel Ainsworth, March 4, 1894.
25. Blevins, ed., p. 51.
26. Schlesinger, ed., p. 394.

The New Glen Eyrie

1.   H.R. Brands, T.R.:The Last Romantic, p. 367.
2.   John Fisher, A Builder of the West, p. 309.
3.   Marshall Sprague, Newport in the Rockies, p. 134.
4.   Dorothy Carr's diary, December 18, 1902.
5.   Ibid, December 23, 1902.
6.   Ibid, January 3, 1903.
7.   Ibid, May 4, 1903.
8.   Ibid, June 6, 1903.
9.   Peter Harrison to Elsie Palmer, July 31, 1903.
10. Dorothy Palmer to David Mckibbin, February 5, 1949.
11. Peter Harrison to Elsie Palmer, October 21, 1903.
12. Ibid, November 23, 1903.
13. Ibid, July 31, 1903.
14. Sterner moved to New York in 1906 and transformed the architecture in Greenwich Village.
15. Quoted in Tim Blevins, ed., Legends, Labors and Loves, p. 230.
16. Rhoda Wilcox, The Man on The Iron Horse, p. 45.
17. Sprague, p. 264.
18. Fisher, p. 310.

19. Ibid.
20. Lubow, p. 209.
21. Hamlin Garland, Daughter of the Middle Border, pp. 229–230.

My Kingdom for a Horse

1.   Tim Blevins, ed., Legends, Labors and Loves, p. 222.
2.   WJP to Cecelia Jacobeit, November 17, 1906.
3.   Dorothy Black Spann, Black Pioneers, p. 54.
4.   Quoted in Blevins, ed. p. 317.
5.   Ibid, p. 294.
6.   Ibid, p. 285.
7.   New York Times, February 25, 1907, p. 15.
8.   Marshall Sprague, Newport in the Rockies, p.144.
9.   Ibid, pp. 144–145.
10. Ibid, p. 145.
11. Ibid.
12. Blevins. ed., p, 279.
13. Sprague, p. 146.
14. Blevins, ed., p. 295.
15. Ibid, p. 285.
16. Ibid, p. 286.
17. Ibid, p. 283.
18. Sprague, p. 148.
19. Blevins, ed., p. 311.
20. Ibid, p. 312.
21. Arthur Schlesinger, Jr., ed., Almanac of American History, p. 404.
22. Ibid, p. 416.
23. John Fisher, A Builder of the West, p. 318.

Epilogue: Glen Eyrie and Beyond

1.   Quoted in Tim Blevins, ed., Legends, Labors and Loves, p. 332.
2.   Ibid, pp. 338–339.
3.   L.H. Myers, The Root and the Flower, p. 201.
4.   Ibid, p. 8.

Select Bibliography

Bailey, Ralph Edgar. *Fight for the Royal Gorge*. New York: William Morrow, 1968.

Bell, William. *New Tracks in North America*. London: Chapman and Hall, 1869.

Black, Celeste. *Queen of Glen Eyrie*. Colorado Springs: Nav Press, 2008.

Blevins, Tim, ed. *Legends, Labors, amd Loves of William Jackson Palmer*. Colorado Springs: Pikes Peak Library District, 2009.

Carr, Alice Comyns. *Reminiscences*. London: Hutchinson and Compnay, 1926.

Clothier, Isaac. *Letters*. Philadelphia, 1906.

Fisher, John. *A Builder of the West*. Caldwell, Idaho: Caxton, 1939.

Garland, Hamlin. *A Daughter of the Middle Border*. New York: Grosset and Dunlap, 1922.

Hayes, Alexa. *"Coning Elsie Palmer."* Honors Thesis. Atlanta: Emory University, 2010.

Howbert, Irving. *Memories of a Lifetime in the Pikes Peak Region*. New York: Putnam, 1926.

Kaplan, Fred. *Henry James*. Baltimore: Johns Hopkins University Press, 1992.

Kingsley, Rose. *South By West*. London: W. Ibister and Co., 1874.

Knightley, Philip. *The First Casualty*. New York: Harcourt Brace, 1975.

Lubow, Arthur. *The Reporter Who Would Be King.* New York: Scribner's, 2001.

Myers, L.H. *The Root and the Flower.* New York: New York Review of Books. 2001.

Ormond, Richard. *Sargent.* Princeton, NJ: Princeton University Press, 1998.

Schlesinger, Arthur, Jr., ed. *Almanac of American History.* Greenwich, CT: Barnes and Noble, 1993.

Sprague, Marshall. *Newport in the Rockies.* Fourth Edition. Athens, Ohio: Ohio University Press, 1987.

Stone, Irving. *Men to Match My Mountains.* New York: Doubleday, 1956.

Wilcox, Rhoda. *The Man on the Iron Horse.* Colorado Springs: Denton Printing Co., 1959.

Wolcott, Frances. Heritage of Years. New York: Minton, Balch and Co., 1932.

Letters, Diaries, and Journals

William Jackson Palmer Collection, Timothy Nicholson Collection, and Elsie Queen Nicholson Collection, Colorado Springs Pioneers Museum, Starsmore Center for Local History. Colorado Springs, Colorado.

Index